# Vocabulary Building Practice and Apply: Grade 6

### BY
### MARILYN K. SMITH AND VICTORIA QUIGLEY FORBES

COPYRIGHT © 2001 Mark Twain Media, Inc.

ISBN 1-58037-157-4

Printing No. CD-1378

Mark Twain Media, Inc., Publishers
Distributed by Carson-Dellosa Publishing Company, Inc.

# Table of Contents

# Introduction to the Teacher

Vocabulary words are an important part of our language. They are a part of our everyday listening, reading, and writing. Vocabulary words are often categorized to help with student learning. Student comprehension of vocabulary meaning is heightened when the words are related to a certain topic or theme. Each unit in this book includes a list of vocabulary words based on such a topic or theme. This will help the students understand and use the words more effectively.

Each unit incorporates an *Introduction* page, a *Get the Facts* page, a *Skills and Practice* page, and a *Vocabulary Quiz*. All pages are reproducible for student use.

Introduction - This page includes the topic and a short paragraph elaborating on that topic. There is also a list of words with pronunciations for the unit. This page will help the teacher to introduce the words and the topic and generate further discussion.

Get the Facts - This page is intended for the use of each student to learn the meaning of the words and as a resource for the skills and practice page that follows.

Skills and Practice - Many units include a synonym and antonym activity and/or categorizing. This allows the student to show mastery of the meaning of the words, as well as generate new words that are related. There are also activities to help take the student beyond the meaning of the words in the "Extend Your Vocabulary" section.

Vocabulary Quiz - This page may be used to test the students' knowledge of the words.

All units can be used in order or in isolation with a certain theme or topic. A list of more vocabulary words, as well as answer keys, is also provided at the end of the book. There are also forms that can be used with any unit and any vocabulary word. A list page, Venn diagram, and T-Chart are included to use with various Extend Your Vocabulary activities.

Criteria for the vocabulary words selected for this book included *The Basic Skills Word List, The New Reading Teachers Book of Lists, Words to Use for Sentence Building*, and numerous thesauruses. Words were most importantly chosen based on the word's appropriateness to grade level and lesson, theme, or topic. A combination of 40 years of teaching by the authors of the book at this grade level also contributed to the selection of the words.

iii

# Pronunciation Key

| a | hat | îr | here | o͝o | look, put | ch | child |
| ā | age | ī | ice | o͞o | tool | ng | long |
| ä | far | i | it | ou | out | sh | she |
| e | let | o | hot | oi | oil | th | thin |
| ē | equal | ō | open | u | cup | *th* | those |
| ər | term | ô | law, order | ū, yo͞o | use | zh | measure |
| âr | care | | | ü | rule | | |

ə
— a    in about
— e    in taken
— i    in pencil
— o    in lemon
— u    in circus

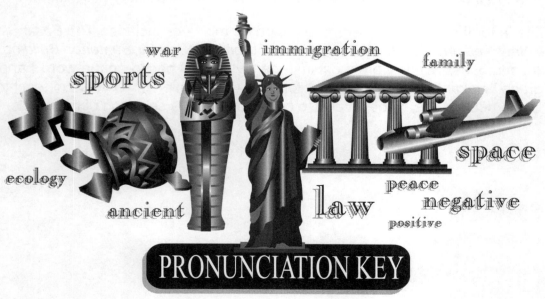

PRONUNCIATION KEY

# Unit 1: Africa

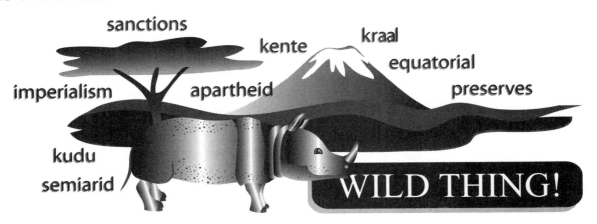

The continent of Africa is very diverse. It includes grasslands and tropical forests and is 40 percent desert. Africa has young mountain ranges and many rivers and streams. Africa is full of customs, cultures, legends, and lore; these differ according to the location of people in Africa. There are many legends on how the animals of Africa came to be; particularly there are many legends about the spider.

equatorial (ek´ wə tôr´ ē əl)

rapids (rap´ ids)

preserve (pri zûrv´)

okapi (ō kä´ pē)

imperialism (im pir´ ē əl iz´ əm)

boycott (boi´ kot´)

sanctions (sangk´ shənz)

kente (ken´ tā)

thatch (thach)

kraal (kräl)

ivory (ī´ və rē)

kudu (ko͞o´ do͞o)

soapstone (sōp´ stōn)

rift valley (rift val´ ē)

semiarid (sem´ ē ar´ id)

lute (lo͞ot)

Pygmy (pig´ mē)

missionary (mish´ ən er´ ē)

apartheid (ə pär´ tīd)

loom (lo͞om)

integral (in´ tə grəl)

gourd (gôrd)

headdress (hed´ dres´)

terra cotta (ter´ ə kot´ ə)

mancala (man cäl´ ə)

# Unit 1: Africa: *Get the Facts!*

**equatorial** (ek´ wə tôr´ ē əl) of, at, or near the equator. *The equator runs through equatorial Africa.*

**rift valley** (rift val´ ē) a long, steep-sided valley lying between two parallel faults. *In Africa there is a series of rift valleys.*

**rapids** (rap´ ids) part of a river's course where the water rushes quickly, often over rocks near the surface. *It is dangerous for a boat in the rapids.*

**semiarid** (sem´ ē ar´ id) having very little rainfall. *Some semiarid grasslands are located in Africa.*

**preserve** (pri zûrv´) a place where wild animals, fish, trees, or plants are protected. *There are wildlife preserves in Africa.*

**lute** (lo͞ot) a musical instrument having a pear-shaped body with six pairs of strings. *The lute was played by the people of Northeast Africa.*

**okapi** (ō kä´ pē) an African mammal that is related to the giraffe but is smaller, without spots, and has a much shorter neck. *The okapis are strange-looking animals.*

**Pygmy** (pig´ mē) one of a group of people of Africa who are less than five feet tall. *The tribe of Pygmies lives in the rain forest.*

**imperialism** (im pir´ ē əl iz´ əm) the extension of a country's power over other lands by military, political, or economic means. *Imperialism involved European nations ruling third-world colonies.*

**missionary** (mish´ ən er´ ē) a person who tries to spread his or her religion to others with different beliefs. *David Livingston was a famous missionary from Scotland who went to Africa.*

**boycott** (boi´ kot´) a special kind of protest in which a group of people refuses to buy or use goods that were produced by another group. *There were boycotts in Africa against the colonial governments.*

**apartheid** (ə pär´ tīd) a policy of South African government that was designed to keep the races separate and unequal. *Apartheid separated the people of South Africa.*

**sanctions** (sangk´ shənz) actions such as boycotts taken by one or more countries to keep certain benefits from another country. *The United States called for sanctions against South Africa.*

**loom** (lo͞om) a machine for weaving thread into cloth. *He moved colorful threads across the loom.*

**kente** (ken´ tā) a brightly colored cloth that is woven by the Asante and Ewe peoples of West Africa. *Kente cloth is woven with hundreds of different patterns.*

**integral** (in´ tə grəl) necessary to make something complete; essential. *Religion and beliefs are an integral part of African life.*

**thatch** (thach) straw or palm leaves, for example, used as a roof or covering. *Some dwellings have thatched roofs.*

**gourd** (gôrd) any of various fleshy fruits that grow on vines and are related to squash. *Some gourds were carved into instruments.*

**kraal** (kräl) a South African village, usually surrounded by a stockade; a fenced pen for cattle or sheep. *The kraal was surrounded by a high fence for protection.*

**headdress** (hed´ dres´) covering or decoration for the head. *A gele is a wrapped headdress worn by African women.*

**ivory** (ī´ və rē) a hard, white substance of which tusks of elephants and walruses are composed. *The average size of an elephant's ivory tusks is about six feet long.*

**terra cotta** (ter´ ə kot´ ə) a kind of hard, brownish-red earthenware used for items such as statues or vases; clay. *The terra cotta figures were made by West Africans.*

**kudu** (ko͞o´ do͞o) a large, grayish-brown African antelope with white stripes. *The kudu was about four and a half feet tall at the shoulder.*

**mancala** (man cäl´ ə) an African game in which two players move pieces from one cup to another until there are no more moves. *The natives carved beautiful boards for the game mancala.*

**soapstone** (sōp´ stōn) a soft rock that feels like soap, used for griddles or hearths, for example. *Some Africans carve soapstone into figures and utensils.*

Name: _____ Date: _____

# Unit 1: Africa: *Skills and Practice*

**Directions:** For each word give a **synonym** from the vocabulary word list below. A **synonym** is a word that means the same or nearly the same.

| | | | | |
|---|---|---|---|---|
| **lute** | **kente** | **mancala** | **gourd** | **headdress** |
| **thatch** | **ivory** | **soapstone** | **kudu** | **sanctions** |
| **okapi** | **integral** | **terra cotta** | **boycott** | |

1. straw _____

2. necessary _____

3. instrument _____

4. mammal _____

5. antelope _____

6. cloth _____

7. rock _____

8. game _____

9. clay _____

10. squash _____

11. tusks _____

12. gele _____

13. protest _____

_____

> **Did You Know?** Clapping was a gesture of thanks when receiving a gift in Africa; no matter how small the gift, it was received with both hands. This symbolized that it was a generous gift.

**Directions:** Write a sentence for the following words on your own paper. Remember to check your spelling and punctuation.

| | | | | |
|---|---|---|---|---|
| **missionary** | **equatorial** | **rift valley** | **rapids** | **semiarid** |
| **preserve** | **Pygmy** | **loom** | **apartheid** | **kraal** |
| **imperialism** | | | | |

## Extend Your Vocabulary

1. Make a list of all the African countries.
2. Compare and contrast two countries in Africa; include things such as customs and religion.
3. Research the importance of the Nile River.
4. Make a ceremonial African mask. Use a variety of materials.

Name: _____   Date: _____

# Unit 1: Africa: *Vocabulary Quiz*

**Directions:** Match each vocabulary word with the correct meaning. Write the word on the line next to the meaning.

| | | | | |
|---|---|---|---|---|
| **equatorial** | **rift valley** | **rapids** | **semiarid** | **preserve** |
| **lute** | **okapi** | **Pygmy** | **imperialism** | **missionary** |
| **boycott** | **apartheid** | **sanctions** | **loom** | **kente** |
| **integral** | **thatch** | **gourd** | **kraal** | **headdress** |
| **ivory** | **terra cotta** | **kudu** | **mancala** | **soapstone** |

1. _____ straw or palm leaves, for example, used as a roof or covering

2. _____ a long, steep-sided valley lying between two parallel faults

3. _____ actions such as boycotts taken by one or more countries to keep certain benefits from another country

4. _____ part of a river's course where the water rushes quickly, often over rocks near the surface

5. _____ covering or decoration for the head

6. _____ an African mammal that is related to the giraffe but is smaller, without spots, and has a much shorter neck

7. _____ a machine for weaving thread into cloth

8. _____ of, at, or near the equator

9. _____ kind of hard, brownish-red earthenware used for statues or vases

10. _____ the extension of a country's power over other lands by military, political, or economic means

11. _____ a brightly colored cloth woven by the Asante and Ewe peoples

12. _____ having very little rainfall

13. _____ a large, grayish-brown African antelope with white stripes

14. _____ a special kind of protest when a group of people refuses to buy or use goods produced by another group

15. _____ necessary to make something complete; essential

16. _____ a place where wild animals, fish, trees, or plants are protected

17. _____ a South African village, usually surrounded by a stockade; a fenced pen for cattle or sheep

18. _____ a musical instrument having a pear-shaped body with six pairs of strings

19. _____ any of various fleshy fruits that grow on vines and are related to squash

20. _____ a person who tries to spread his or her religion to others with different beliefs

21. _____ an African game

22. _____ a policy of South African government that was designed to keep the races separate and unequal

23. _____ a hard, white substance of which tusks of elephants or walruses are composed

24. _____ one of a group of people of Africa who are less than five feet tall

25. _____ a soft rock that feels like soap

## Unit 2: Mysteries

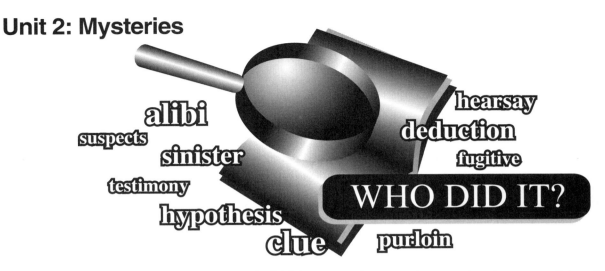

A mystery is something that is hidden or unknown. It can also be something that is not explained or understood. A mystery is one of the most popular types of fiction enjoyed by children and adults. A mystery story is mainly a puzzle rather than a detective story. Mysteries often include several suspects, a crime, a motive, and the opportunity to commit the crime. Mysteries involve a character, usually a detective, who solves the mystery.

alibi (al´ ə bī´)

deduction (di duk´ shən)

red herring (red her´ ing)

suspects (sus´ pekts´)

ciphers (sī´ fərs)

analyzing (an´ ə līz´ ing)

fugitive (fyoo´ ji tiv)

hypothesis (hī poth´ ə sis)

eavesdropper (ēvz´ drop´ ər)

admonition (ad´ mə nish´ ən)

hearsay (hir´ sā´)

disclosure (dis klō´ zhər)

hunch (hunch)

clue (kloo)

sinister (sin´ is tər)

sleuth (slooth)

witness (wit´ nis)

disguise (dis gīz´)

strategies (strat´ ə jēs)

appraise (ə prāz´)

testimony (tes´ tə mō´ nē)

newsmonger (nooz´ män´ gər)

breakthrough (brāk´ throo´)

purloin (pər loin´)

aloof (ə loof´)

5

# Unit 2: Mysteries: *Get the Facts!*

**alibi** (al´ ə bī´) a suspect's claim that he or she was not near the crime scene at the time of the crime. *The butler had an alibi for the night of the crime.*

**clue** (klо̄о̄) something that appears to lead the detective a step closer to solving the crime, mystery, or problem. *The police officer could find no fingerprints or clues.*

**deduction** (di duk´ shən) using the facts to infer a conclusion; inference. *The detective reached her deduction by studying the facts.*

**sinister** (sin´ is tər) bad; evil; dishonest. *The criminal had a sinister plan.*

**red herring** (red her´ ing) a false clue that misleads a detective in an investigation. *Red herrings in a mystery heighten the suspense.*

**sleuth** (slооth) detective. *The sleuth on the case was very precise with details.*

**suspects** (sus´ pekts´) the people who are connected to the crime in some way and appear to have a motive for committing the crime. *The police arrested three suspects in the robbery.*

**witness** (wit´ nis) a person who discovers a crime, or has some kind of information about the crime. *The inspector interviewed all the witnesses.*

**ciphers** (sī´ fərs) secret writings; codes. *Parts of the letter were in ciphers.*

**disguise** (dis gīz´) use of changes in clothes or appearance to hide who one really is or to look like someone else. *Detectives sometimes use disguises.*

**analyzing** (an´ ə līz´ ing) examining carefully and in detail. *The inspector was analyzing all the clues.*

**strategies** (strat´ ə jēs) the skillful planning and management of anything. *The investigator used many strategies to locate the missing person.*

**fugitive** (fyoo´ ji tiv) person who is running away or who has run away. *The criminal became a fugitive from the law.*

**appraise** (ə prāz´) estimate the value or amount. *The stolen diamond necklace had been appraised to be worth thousands.*

**hypothesis** (hī poth´ ə sis) something assumed because it seems likely to be a true explanation; theory. *The detective acted on the hypothesis that she was innocent.*

**testimony** (tes´ tə mō´ nē) statement used for evidence or proof. *The testimony of the witness convicted the criminal.*

**eavesdropper** (ēvz´ drop´ ər) person who listens to talk he or she is not supposed to hear or listens secretly to a private conversation. *The maid was an eavesdropper to the conversation between her employer and his wife.*

**newsmonger** (nooz´ män´ gər) a gossip. *The newsmonger destroyed the man's reputation.*

**admonition** (ad´ mə nish´ ən) gentle reproof or warning. *The secretary received an admonition from the detective for not telling him all the information at the beginning of the investigation.*

**breakthrough** (brāk´ throo´) the solution of some baffling problem. *The last clue was a breakthrough in the case.*

**hearsay** (hir´ sā´) common talk; gossip or rumor. *The story was just hearsay.*

**purloin** (pər loin´) steal. *What did the robber purloin from the jewelry store?*

**disclosure** (dis klō´ zhər) something disclosed; open to view; made known. *The newspaper's disclosures shocked the people.*

**aloof** (ə loof´) indifferent; reserved; tending to keep to oneself. *His manner was cool and aloof.*

**hunch** (hunch) a vague feeling of suspicion. *I had a hunch about the identity of the robber.*

Name: _____ Date: _____

# Unit 2: Mysteries: *Skills and Practice*

**Directions:** For each word give a **synonym** from the vocabulary word list below. A **synonym** is a word that means the same or nearly the same.

| | | | | | |
|---|---|---|---|---|---|
| **aloof** | **clue** | **fugitive** | **deduction** | **testimony** | **ciphers** |
| **sleuth** | **witness** | **admonition** | **hypothesis** | **sinister** | **hearsay** |
| **appraise** | **analyzing** | **purloin** | | | |

1. hint _____
3. detective _____
5. evil _____
7. theory _____
9. estimate _____
11. steal _____
13. runaway _____
15. observer _____

2. inference _____
4. warning _____
6. codes _____
8. examining _____
10. rumor _____
12. indifferent _____
14. deposition _____

**Did You Know?** The first Sherlock Homes mystery, *A Study in Scarlet*, written by Sir Arthur Conan Doyle, was published in 1887. It was so successful that Doyle gave up his medical practice to write full-time.

**Directions:** Write an **antonym** from the list of vocabulary words below on the line next to each word. An **antonym** is a word that means the opposite or nearly opposite.

**breakthrough**        **disclosure**

1. concealment _____
2. problem _____

**Directions:** Write a sentence for the following words on your own paper. Remember to check your spelling and punctuation.

| | | | |
|---|---|---|---|
| **alibi** | **red herring** | **suspects** | **newsmonger** |
| **hunch** | **eavesdropper** | **strategies** | **disguise** |

## Extend Your Vocabulary

1. Hide an object in the classroom. Make a list of clues for a classmate to locate the object.
2. Make a list of famous detectives.
3. Imagine that you are at the scene of a crime. Write about what you might hear, smell, or see.
4. As a class, research a famous mystery author. Write a report about him or her.

Name: _____    Date: _____

# Unit 2: Mysteries: *Vocabulary Quiz*

**Directions:** Match each vocabulary word with the correct meaning. Write the word on the line next to the meaning.

| | | | | |
|---|---|---|---|---|
| alibi | clue | deduction | sinister | red herring |
| sleuth | suspects | witness | ciphers | disguise |
| analyzing | strategies | fugitive | appraise | hypothesis |
| testimony | eavesdropper | newsmonger | admonition | breakthrough |
| hearsay | purloin | disclosure | aloof | hunch |

1. _____ statement used for evidence or proof

2. _____ a suspect's claim that he or she was not near the crime scene at the time of the crime

3. _____ something assumed because it seems likely to be a true explanation; theory

4. _____ the person who discovers a crime or has some kind of information about the crime

5. _____ something disclosed; open to view; made known

6. _____ secret writings; codes

7. _____ estimate the value or amount

8. _____ false clue that misleads a detective in an investigation

9. _____ gentle reproof or warning

10. _____ the people who are connected to the crime in some way and appear to have a motive for committing the crime

11. _____ person who listens to talk he or she is not supposed to hear or listens secretly to a private conversation

12. _____ something that appears to lead the detective closer to solving the crime, mystery, or problem

13. _____ common talk; gossip or rumor

14. _____ use of changes in clothes or appearance to hide who one really is or to look like someone else

15. _____ vague feeling of suspicion

16. _____ skillful planning and management of anything

17. _____ a gossip

18. _____ using the facts to infer a conclusion; inference

19. _____ solution of some baffling problem

20. _____ detective

21. _____ indifferent; reserved; tending to keep to oneself

22. _____ bad; evil; dishonest

23. _____ steal

24. _____ examining carefully and in detail

25. _____ person who is running away or who has run away

# Unit 3: Family

Family is defined as a person's relatives. Families can be large or small. Family includes immediate family members such as mother, father, and siblings, as well as extended family. Extended family includes aunts, uncles, and grandparents. Often families are alike in many ways. Sometimes siblings and cousins look very much alike. Many families share traditions passed on from generation to generation.

compatible (kəm pat´ ə bəl)

matrimony (ma´ trə mō´ nē)

generation (jen´ ər ā´ shən)

offspring (ôf´ spring´)

ancestry (an´ ses´ trē)

parentage (par´ ənt ij)

sibling (sib´ ling)

fraternity (frə tərn´ ət ē)

accommodating (ə kom´ ə dāt´ ing)

congenial (kən jēn´ yəl)

reciprocal (ri sip´ rə kəl)

genealogy (jē´ nē äl´ ə jē)

continuous (kən tin´ yōō əs)

domestic (də mes´ tik)

spouse (spous)

reunion (rē yōōn´ yən)

commitment (kə mit´ mənt)

lineage (lin´ ē ij)

alliance (ə lī´ əns)

kindred (kin´ drid)

mutual (myōō´ chōō əl)

reconciliation (rek´ ən sil´ ē ā´ shən)

complementary (kom´ plə men´ tə rē)

nourishing (nər´ ish ing)

race (rās)

# Unit 3: Family: *Get the Facts!*

**compatible** (kəm pat′ ə bəl) able to exist with or get along well together; in agreement. *My cousin and I are quite compatible.*

**domestic** (də mes′ tik) of the home, household, or family affairs. *All the members of Maria's family help with the domestic chores.*

**matrimony** (ma′ trə mō′ nē) marriage. *They are celebrating 50 years of matrimony.*

**spouse** (spous) husband or wife. *The spouses were invited to accompany their husbands on the cruise.*

**generation** (jen′ ər ā′ shən) all the people born at about the same time. *My parents' generation is almost all retired.*

**reunion** (rē yōon′ yən) a social gathering of persons who have been separated for some time. *We have a large family reunion every year.*

**offspring** (ôf′ spring′) the young of a person, animal, or plant; descendant. *All of his offspring resembled him.*

**commitment** (kə mit′ mənt) pledge; promise. *A couple makes a commitment to each other when they get married.*

**ancestry** (an′ ses′ trē) line of descent from ancestors; lineage. *The princess was to marry someone of noble ancestry.*

**lineage** (lin′ ē ij) descent in a direct line from an ancestor. *She researched her lineage in order to write the book about her family.*

**parentage** (par′ ənt ij) descent from parents; family line. *Her parentage showed many family members she did not know.*

**alliance** (ə lī′ əns) a union of persons or groups formed by agreement for some special purpose. *The families in the neighborhood formed an alliance against crime.*

**sibling** (sib′ ling) brother or sister. *I had nine siblings in my large family.*

**kindred** (kin′ drid) like; similar; related. *The two friends felt they were kindred spirits.*

**fraternity** (frə tərn′ ət ē) group having the same interests or type of work; brotherhood. *The fraternity shared many aspects of their lives.*

**mutual** (myōo′ chōo əl) done, felt, or said by one toward the other; shared in common. *We had mutual goals before we were married.*

**accommodating** (ə kom′ ə dāt′ ing) willing to do favors; obliging. *My aunt and uncle were very accommodating when I visited them.*

**reconciliation** (rek′ ən sil′ ē ā′ shən) settlement or adjustment of disagreements or differences. *A reconciliation between the mother and daughter was needed.*

**congenial** (kən jēn′ yəl) having similar tastes and interests; getting on well together. *My sister and I are very congenial in many ways.*

**complementary** (kom′ plə men′ tə rē) completing or making perfect. *The addition of the boy to the family was complementary.*

**reciprocal** (ri sip′ rə kəl) in return. *I did not expect a reciprocal gift from my brother for my birthday.*

**nourishing** (nər′ ish ing) keeping well-fed and healthy. *The mother provided a nourishing meal for her children.*

**genealogy** (jē′ nē äl′ ə jē) account of the descent of a person or family from an ancestor. *She studied her great-grandfather's genealogy.*

**race** (rās) persons, animals, or plants having the same ancestors. *The human race is very diverse.*

**continuous** (kən tin′ yōo əs) without a stop or break; connected; unbroken. *There was a continuous line of cousins in the reunion picture.*

Name: _____     Date: _____

# Unit 3: Family: *Skills and Practice*

**Directions:** For each word give a **synonym** from the vocabulary word list below. A **synonym** is a word that means the same or nearly the same.

| | | | | |
|---|---|---|---|---|
| **matrimony** | **lineage** | **spouse** | **offspring** | **accommodating** |
| **sibling** | **kindred** | **mutual** | **commitment** | **reconciliation** |
| **alliance** | | | | |

1. marriage _____        2. wife _____

3. promise _____        4. ancestry _____

5. brother _____        6. obliging _____

7. related _____        8. same _____

9. forgiveness _____       10. union _____

11. litter _____

**Did You Know?** On January 6, French families eat a special dinner together. The children eat slices of a flat almond pie called a *galette.* A charm is hidden in one of the slices. Whoever finds the charm is crowned king or queen for the night.

**Directions:** Write an **antonym** from the list of vocabulary words below on the line next to each word. An **antonym** is a word that means the opposite or nearly opposite.

| | | | |
|---|---|---|---|
| **nourishing** | **domestic** | **continuous** | **compatible** |

1. disagreeing _____     2. starving _____

3. broken _____          4. wild _____

**Directions:** Write a sentence for the following words on your own paper. Remember to check your spelling and punctuation.

| | | | | |
|---|---|---|---|---|
| **generation** | **reunion** | **parentage** | **complementary** | **race** |
| **congenial** | **genealogy** | **reciprocal** | **fraternity** | |

### Extend Your Vocabulary

1. Research your family genealogy and make a family tree.
2. Write a narrative piece about a reunion you have attended.
3. Write a persuasive piece about why it is better to be the oldest, middle, or youngest child in your family.
4. Make a list of ways to be compatible with your siblings.

Name: _____ Date: _____

# Unit 3: Family: *Vocabulary Quiz*

**Directions:** Match each vocabulary word with the correct meaning. Write the word on the line next to the meaning.

| | | | | |
|---|---|---|---|---|
| **compatible** | **domestic** | **matrimony** | **spouse** | **generation** |
| **reunion** | **offspring** | **commitment** | **ancestry** | **lineage** |
| **parentage** | **alliance** | **sibling** | **fraternity** | **kindred** |
| **mutual** | **nourishing** | **genealogy** | **congenial** | **complementary** |
| **reconciliation** | **reciprocal** | **race** | **continuous** | **accommodating** |

1. _____ willing to do favors; obliging

2. _____ of the home, household, or family affairs

3. _____ group having the same interests or kind of work; brotherhood

4. _____ the young of a person, animal, or plant; descendant

5. _____ keeping well-fed and healthy

6. _____ descent from parents; family line

7. _____ without a stop or break; connected; unbroken

8. _____ brother or sister

9. _____ done, felt, or said by one toward the other; shared in common

10. _____ marriage

11. _____ having similar tastes and interests; getting on well together

12. _____ a pledge; promise

13. _____ settlement or adjustment of disagreements or differences

14. _____ husband or wife

15. _____ like; similar; related

16. _____ able to exist or get along well together; in agreement

17. _____ in return

18. _____ line of descent from ancestors; lineage

19. _____ persons, animals, or plants having the same ancestors

20. _____ a union of persons or groups formed by agreement for some special purpose

21. _____ completing or making perfect

22. _____ all the people born at about the same time

23. _____ account of the descent of a person or family from an ancestor

24. _____ a social gathering of persons who have been separated or who have interests in common

25. _____ descent in a direct line from an ancestor

# Unit 4: Business

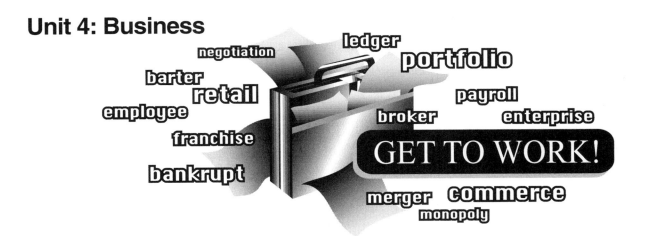

Business deals with buying and selling, commercial dealings, and trade. Items can be bought, sold, or traded at wholesale or retail prices. Businessmen and women work many different hours. They often work together on a project or transaction. Each businessman or woman may have a different and specialized job. Some businesses are large companies made up of smaller companies owned by a group of people; other companies may be run by one owner.

barter (bärt´ ər)

franchise (fran´ chīz´)

merger (mûr´ jər)

transaction (tran zak´ shən)

bankrupt (bangk´ rupt´)

agenda (ə jen´ də)

portfolio (pôrt fō´ lē ō´)

negotiation (ni gō´ shē ā´ shən)

interchange (in´ tər chānj´)

retail (rē´ tāl´)

workmanship (wûrk´ mən ship´)

payroll (pā´ rōl´)

Rolodex (rō´ lə deks´)

commerce (kom´ ərs)

inventory (in´ ven tôr´ ē)

monopoly (mə nop´ ə lē)

vendor (ven´ dər)

pursuit (pər sōōt´)

errand (er´ ənd)

broker (brō´ k ər)

employee (em ploi´ ē)

wholesale (hōl´ sāl´)

maneuver (mə nōō´ vər)

enterprise (ent´ ər prīz´)

ledger (lej´ ər)

# Unit 4: Business: *Get the Facts!*

**barter** (bärt´ ər) to trade by exchanging one kind of goods for other goods without using money. *The Indian bartered furs with the trappers.*

**commerce** (kom´ ərs) the buying and selling of goods between different places, especially in large amounts. *The teacher instructed the class about business and commerce.*

**franchise** (fran´ chīz´) privilege of selling products of a manufacturer in a given area. *He bought the franchise to the popular restaurant.*

**inventory** (in´ ven tôr´ ē) all the articles listed or to be listed; stock. *They took inventory all night before the big sale.*

**merger** (mûr´ jər) combination; consolidation. *The larger company was the result of a merger of three smaller companies.*

**monopoly** (mə nop´ ə lē) the exclusive control of a commodity or service. *The company has a monopoly in its area of business.*

**transaction** (tran zak´ shən) piece of business. *The transaction was recorded on tape.*

**vendor** (ven´ dər) seller; peddler. *The vendor comes once a month to sell his goods.*

**bankrupt** (bangk´ rupt´) unable to pay one's debts. *The businessmen were worried about going bankrupt.*

**pursuit** (pər sōot´) that which one does as a profession or recreation; occupation. *Selling has always been her favorite pursuit.*

**agenda** (ə jen´ də) list of things to be dealt with or done. *The stockholders went over the agenda for the annual meeting.*

**errand** (er´ ənd) what one is sent to do. *One of my jobs as secretary is to run errands for the office.*

**portfolio** (pôrt fō´ lē ō´) a portable case for carrying loose papers or materials; briefcase. *The important report was in her portfolio.*

**broker** (brō´ kər) person who buys and sells stocks, bonds, and securities for other people. *I need to return a call to my broker.*

**negotiation** (ni gō´ shē ā´ shən) an arrangement. *Negotiations between the business and its employees are almost complete.*

**employee** (em ploi´ ē) person who works for another person or firm for pay. *The employee was late for work again.*

**interchange** (in´ tər chānj´) give and take; exchange. *We interchanged our ideas at the meeting.*

**wholesale** (hōl´ sāl´) sale of goods in large quantities at a time, usually to those who will, in turn, sell them to consumers. *We buy paper goods wholesale.*

**retail** (rē´ tāl´) sale of goods in small quantities directly to the consumer. *We bought the coat at retail price.*

**maneuver** (mə nōo´ vər) a skillful plan or movement. *We had to maneuver carefully in the crowded room.*

**workmanship** (wûrk´ mən ship´) the art or skill of a worker or the work done. *His workmanship required years of practice.*

**enterprise** (ent´ ər prīz´) an undertaking or project. *Hopefully the business enterprise will be a success.*

**payroll** (pā´ rōl´) list of persons to be paid and the amount that each one is to receive. *She is in charge of the payroll.*

**ledger** (lej´ ər) book of accounts in which a business keeps a record of all money transactions. *Jason laid the ledger near his computer.*

**Rolodex** (rō´ lə deks´) a trademark for an item that functions as a desktop rotary file of removable cards for names, addresses, and telephone numbers. *He looked up her address in his Rolodex.*

Name: _____ Date: _____

# Unit 4: Business: *Skills and Practice*

**Directions:** For each word give a **synonym** from the vocabulary word list below. A **synonym** is a word that means the same or nearly the same.

| | | | | |
|---|---|---|---|---|
| **pursuit** | **agenda** | **negotiation** | **inventory** | **barter** |
| **vendor** | **errand** | **merger** | **portfolio** | **interchange** |

1. trade _____
3. arrangement _____
5. seller _____
7. briefcase _____
9. syllabus _____

2. stock _____
4. occupation _____
6. exchange _____
8. consolidation _____
10. task _____

**Did You Know?** James Ritty was the inventor of the cash register. He invented it in 1879 for his saloon in Ohio.

**Directions:** Write an **antonym** from the list of vocabulary words below on the line next to each word. An **antonym** is a word that means the opposite or nearly opposite.

| | | | |
|---|---|---|---|
| **bankrupt** | **employee** | **monopoly** | **retail** |

1. wholesale _____
3. solvent _____

2. employer _____
4. free trade _____

**Directions:** Write a sentence for the following words on your own paper. Remember to check your spelling and punctuation.

| | | | | |
|---|---|---|---|---|
| **commerce** | **franchise** | **monopoly** | **transaction** | **Rolodex** |
| **broker** | **maneuver** | **workmanship** | **enterprise** | **payroll** |

### Extend Your Vocabulary

1. Set up a make-believe business. Tell about the details such as supplies, location, jobs, employees, and so on.
2. Make a list of franchises. Research the number one franchise in the United States.
3. Make a monthly expense account on how you spend your allowance. Record all expenses.
4. Make a list of the different people who use a portfolio.

Name: _____ Date: _____

# Unit 4: Business: *Vocabulary Quiz*

**Directions:** Match each vocabulary word with the correct meaning. Write the word on the line next to the meaning.

| | | | | |
|---|---|---|---|---|
| barter | commerce | franchise | inventory | merger |
| monopoly | transaction | vendor | bankrupt | pursuit |
| agenda | errand | portfolio | broker | negotiation |
| employee | interchange | wholesale | retail | maneuver |
| workmanship | enterprise | payroll | ledger | Rolodex |

1. _____ person who buys and sells stocks, bonds, and securities for other people

2. _____ all the articles listed or to be listed; stock

3. _____ sale of goods in small quantities directly to the consumer

4. _____ seller; peddler

5. _____ list of persons to be paid and the amount that each one is to receive

6. _____ what one is sent to do

7. _____ an arrangement

8. _____ to trade by exchanging one kind of goods for other goods without using money

9. _____ sale of goods in large quantities at a time, usually to those who will, in turn, sell them to consumers.

10. _____ the buying and selling of goods between different places, especially in large amounts

11. _____ person who works for another person or firm for pay

12. _____ combination; consolidation

13. _____ the art or skill of a worker or the work done

14. _____ that which one does as a profession, recreation, or occupation

15. _____ a trademark for an item that functions as a desktop rotary file of removable cards for names, addresses, and telephone numbers

16. _____ privilege of selling the products of a manufacturer in a given area

17. _____ give and take; exchange

18. _____ list of things to be dealt with or done

19. _____ a skillful plan or movement

20. _____ the exclusive control of a commodity or service

21. _____ an undertaking or project

22. _____ a portable case for carrying loose papers; briefcase

23. _____ book of accounts in which a business keeps a record of all money transactions

24. _____ unable to pay one's debts

25. _____ piece of business

# Unit 5: World War II

No country suffered greater economic trouble after World War I than Germany. It suffered a depression, factory production was halted, banks closed, and there was great unemployment. Adolf Hitler became dictator and formed an alliance between Italy and Japan. In 1939, Hitler and his local party, the Nazis, brought the world to World War II. Hitler believed in a supreme race that excluded people of Jewish heritage and other minority groups. Terrible destruction of human life resulted. The United States and its allies defeated Hitler, ending six long years of fighting.

relocation (rē lō kā′ shən)

Holocaust (hol′ ə kôst)

Allies (al′ īz)

Nazi (nät′ sē)

Resistance (ri zis′ təns)

swastika (swäs′ ti kə)

ghetto (get′ ō)

home front (hōm′ frunt′)

atrocity (ə tros′ ə tē)

optimistic (op′ tə mis′ tik)

riveter (riv′ it ər)

economic (ek′ ə nom′ ik)

extermination (ek stûr′ mə nā′ shən)

blitzkrieg (blits krēg′)

concentration camp

    (kon′ sən trā′ shən kamp)

Axis (ak′ sis)

compensation (kom′ pən sā′ shən)

atom bomb (at′ əm bom)

deportation (dē′ pôr tā′ shən)

pogrom (pō′ gräm′)

rationing (rash′ ən ing)

anti-Semitism (an′ tī sem′ ə tiz′ əm)

pessimistic (pes′ ə mis′ tik)

scapegoat (skāp′ gōt′)

sabotage (sab′ ə täzh′)

# Unit 5: World War II: *Get the Facts!*

**relocation** (rē lō kā´ shən) move to a new place; locate or settle anew. *Japanese-Americans were forced into relocation camps in 1942.*

**blitzkrieg** (blits krēg´) German word meaning sudden, violent attack using many airplanes and tanks. *Poland was surprised with a blitzkrieg by the Germans.*

**Holocaust** (hol´ ə kôst) mass murder of European Jews by Adolf Hitler and the Nazi Party. *The Holocaust remains a period of brutality in history.*

**concentration camp** (kon´ sən trā´ shən kamp) prison camps established by Adolf Hitler and the Nazi Party for Jews and other political prisoners during World War II. *Concentration camps stand for the worst that humans can do to other humans.*

**Allies** (al´ īz) countries fighting along with the United States against the Axis powers. *One of the U.S. Allies in World War II was Great Britain.*

**Axis** (ak´ sis) the alliance of Germany, Italy, and Japan. *About 70 million people served in either the Allied or Axis armed forces.*

**Nazi** (nät´ sē) member of the German political party called the National Socialist German Workers Party and commanded by Adolf Hitler. *In the 1930s, the Nazis boycotted Jewish businesses.*

**compensation** (kom´ pən sā´ shən) something given to make up for something else. *Congress paid the Japanese-Americans in relocation camps a compensation.*

**Resistance** (ri zis´ təns) people who secretly organize and fight for their freedom in a country occupied and controlled by a foreign power. *About 7,000 Danish Jews were smuggled to safety by the Danish Resistance.*

**atom bomb** (at´ əm bom) powerful weapon created from the splitting of atoms. *The atom bomb was used by President Truman on two Japanese cities, Horoshima and Nagasaki.*

**swastika** (swäs´ ti kə) emblem on the Nazi flag. *The swastika was a cross with the ends bent at right angles.*

**deportation** (de´ pôr tā´ shən) removal from a country by banishment or expulsion. *The deportation of Jews from Germany was Hitler's plan.*

**ghetto** (get´ ō) a part of a city in Europe where Jews were required to live. *A Jewish person was required to live in a ghetto and wear a Star of David emblem.*

**pogrom** (pō´ gräm´) an organized massacre of helpless people. *The pogrom of Jews was a horrendous act.*

**home front** (hōm´ frunt´) term given to the United States mainland during World War II. *World War II affected the American home front.*

**rationing** (rash´ ən ing) to allow only certain amounts of food, gasoline, and other goods to each person. *The United States rationed products such as sugar and flour during World War II.*

**atrocity** (ə tros´ ə tē) very great wickedness or cruelty. *There are acts of atrocity committed in war.*

**anti-Semitism** (an´ tī sem´ ə tiz´ əm) dislike or hatred for Jews; prejudice against Jews. *Anti-Semitism was prevalent during World War II.*

**optimistic** (op´ tə mis´ tik) hoping for the best; inclined to look on the bright side of things. *Anne Frank was an optimistic girl.*

**pessimistic** (pes´ ə mis´ tik) inclined to look on the dark side of things or to see all the difficulties and disadvantages. *The pessimistic man brought the whole group down.*

**riveter** (riv´ it ər) a person in a factory that makes or fastens with rivets. *Rosie the Riveter was the symbol of American women who went to work in factories during the war.*

**scapegoat** (skāp´ gōt´) person or thing made to bear the blame for the mistakes or sins of others. *The Jewish people were the scapegoats of World War II.*

**economic** (ek´ ə nom´ ik) having to do with economics, the science of production, distribution, and consumption of goods and services. *One of the economic conditions for Hitler's rise was large numbers of people who were unemployed.*

**sabotage** (sab´ ə täzh´) damage done by enemy agents or by civilians of a conquered nation. *The Resistance fighters tried to sabotage Hitler's plans.*

**extermination** (ek stûr´ mə nā´ shən) complete destruction. *One phase of Hitler's plan was the extermination of the Jews.*

Name: _____ Date: _____

# Unit 5: World War II: *Skills and Practice*

**Directions:** For each word give a **synonym** from the vocabulary word list below. A **synonym** is a word that means the same or nearly the same.

| | | | |
|---|---|---|---|
| **atom bomb** | **blitzkrieg** | **pogrom** | **compensation** |
| **swastika** | **atrocity** | **sabotage** | |

1. pay _____
2. massacre _____
3. Nazi emblem _____
4. weapon _____
5. cruelty _____
6. damage _____
7. attack _____

---

**Did You Know?** Adolf Hitler succeeded in killing two-thirds of all Jews in Europe before he ended his own life in his bomb-proof bunker under the German Chancellery in Berlin at the end of the war.

---

**Directions:** Write an **antonym** from the list of vocabulary words below on the line next to each word. An **antonym** is a word that means the opposite or nearly opposite.

| | | | |
|---|---|---|---|
| **extermination** | **optimistic** | **allies** | **deportation** |

1. pessimistic _____
2. remain _____
3. create _____
4. enemies _____

**Directions:** Write a sentence for the following words on your own paper. Remember to check your spelling and punctuation.

| | | | | |
|---|---|---|---|---|
| **concentration camp** | **Holocaust** | **relocation** | **riveter** | **Nazi** |
| **anti-Semitism** | **rationing** | **scapegoat** | **ghetto** | **Axis** |
| **home front** | **Resistance** | **economic** | | |

### Extend Your Vocabulary

1. Compare and contrast the causes for World War I and World War II.
2. Research Anne Frank and her role in World War II. Write a report about her.
3. Research Japanese relocation camps. Write a mini-report.
4. Explore World War II through music by listing to the popular songs of that time. How do they reflect the spirit of the people?

Name: _____ Date: _____

# Unit 5: World War II: *Vocabulary Quiz*

**Directions:** Match each vocabulary word with the correct meaning. Write the word on the line next to the meaning.

| | | | | |
|---|---|---|---|---|
| relocation | blitzkrieg | Holocaust | concentration camp | Allies |
| Axis | Nazi | Resistance | compensation | atom bomb |
| swastika | deportation | ghetto | pogrom | home front |
| rationing | optimistic | pessimistic | anti-Semitism | riveter |
| scapegoat | economic | sabotage | extermination | atrocity |

1. _____ to allow only certain amounts of food, gasoline, and other goods to each person

2. _____ move to a new place; locate or settle anew

3. _____ prison camps established by Adolf Hitler and the Nazi Party for Jews and other political prisoners during World War II

4. _____ the alliance of Germany, Italy, and Japan

5. _____ having to do with economics, the science of production, distribution, and consumption of goods and services

6. _____ powerful weapon created from the splitting of atoms

7. _____ hoping for the best; inclined to look on the bright side of things

8. _____ something given to make up for something else

9. _____ complete destruction

10. _____ part of a city in Europe where Jews were required to live

11. _____ term given to the U.S. mainland during the war

12. _____ sudden, violent attack using many airplanes and tanks

13. _____ an organized massacre of helpless people

14. _____ people who secretly organize and fight for their freedom in a country occupied and controlled by a foreign power

15. _____ inclined to look on the dark side of things; to see all the difficulties and disadvantages

16. _____ countries fighting along with the United States against the Axis powers

17. _____ person in a factory that makes or fastens with rivets

18. _____ mass murder of European Jews by Adolf Hitler and the Nazis

19. _____ damage done by enemy agents or by civilians of a conquered nation

20. _____ member of the German political party called the National Socialist German Workers Party

21. _____ dislike or hatred for Jews; prejudice against Jews

22. _____ emblem on the Nazi flag

23. _____ person or thing made to bear the blame for the mistakes or sins of others

24. _____ removal from a country by banishment or expulsion

25. _____ very great wickedness or cruelty

# Unit 6: Ecology

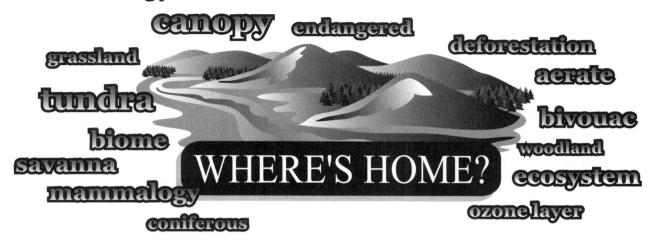

Ecology is the study of living things and their interaction with their home or environment. An environment can be big or small. Earth is the largest environment made up of many smaller environments. The earth is broken down into smaller ecosystems called biomes. Biomes include deserts, tundras, forests, grasslands, and savannas. To keep our ecosystem thriving, we should be concerned with conservation, recycling, pollution, and the ozone layer.

biome (bī´ ōm´)

coniferous (kō nif´ ər əs)

savanna (sə van´ ə)

tundra (tun´ drə)

woodland (wŏod´ lənd)

humus (hyōo´ məs)

conservation (kon´ sər vā´ shən)

dust bowl (dust´ bōl´)

deforestation (dē fôr´ ist ā´ shən)

camouflage (kam´ ə fläzh´)

noxious (nok´ shəs)

ozone layer (ō´ zōn lā´ ər)

bract (brakt)

ecosystem (ek´ ō sis´ təm)

deciduous (dē sij´ ōo əs)

grassland (gras´ land´)

temperate (tem´ pər it)

broad-leaved (brôd´ lēvd´)

mammalogy (ma mal´ ə jē)

endangered (en dān´ jərd)

species (spē´ shēz)

canopy (kan´ ə pē)

understory (un´ dər stôr´ ē)

bivouac (biv´ ōo ak´)

aerate (er´ āt´)

# Unit 6: Ecology: *Get the Facts!*

**biome** (bī´ ōm´) a large geographical area having generally the same climate and vegetation. *What animals are found in the tundra biome?*

**ecosystem** (ek´ ō sis´ təm) a community of interlocking parts that act upon each other in life's grand plan. *The plants and animals interact in an ecosystem.*

**coniferous** (kō nif´ ər əs) bearing cones. *The pine tree is a coniferous tree.*

**deciduous** (dē sij´ oo əs) shedding leaves each year. *Maples, elms, and most oaks are deciduous trees.*

**savanna** (sə van´ ə) a grassy plain with few or no trees. *Savannas are located in the southern United States or near the tropics.*

**grassland** (gras´ land´) land with grass on it, used for pasture. *Grassland vegetation is made up of drought-resistant grasses.*

**tundra** (tun´ drə) a vast, level, treeless plain in the arctic regions. *The ground beneath the tundra surface is frozen in summer.*

**temperate** (tem´ pər it) not very hot and not very cold. *Seattle has a temperate climate.*

**woodland** (wood´ lənd) land covered with trees. *About 29 percent of the United States is woodland.*

**broad-leaved** (brôd´ lēvd´) having broad leaves; leaves that are not needles. *Broad-leaved evergreen forests grow in the United States.*

**humus** (hyoo´ məs) a dark-brown or black part of soil formed from decayed leaves and other vegetable matter. *Humus has valuable plant foods.*

**mammalogy** (ma mal´ ə jē) branch of zoology dealing with mammals. *She was majoring in mammalogy in college.*

**conservation** (kon´ sər vā´ shən) a preserving from harm or decay; protection from loss. *The conservation of our mineral resources is important.*

**endangered** (en dān´ jərd) brought into danger or peril. *The green sea turtle is an endangered animal.*

**dust bowl** (dust´ bōl´) area in the western plains of the United States and Canada where dust storms are frequent and violent. *The dust bowl has long periods of drought with its dry climate.*

**species** (spē´ shēz) groups of animals or plants that have certain permanent characteristics in common and are able to interbreed. *The lion is one species of cat.*

**deforestation** (dē fôr´ ist ā´ shən) removal of trees. *The deforestation of the rain forest has caused many problems.*

**canopy** (kan´ ə pē) green and leafy layer in the rain forest 80–150 feet above the ground, where large, broad leaves catch and block both rain and sunlight. *The canopy has leaves that make a green roof in the tropical rain forest.*

**camouflage** (kam´ ə fläzh´) a disguise or false appearance for the purpose of concealing. *The white fur of a polar bear is a natural camouflage.*

**understory** (un´ dər stôr´ ē) layer that consists of the tops of smaller trees, which receives less light than the canopy. *The understory was studied during our unit on rain forests.*

**noxious** (nok´ shəs) very harmful; poisonous. *King cobra snakes are noxious.*

**bivouac** (biv´ oo ak´) camp outdoors, usually without tents or with very small tents. *They bivouacked in the woods until morning.*

**ozone layer** (ō´ zōn lā´ ər) a protective shield of air high up in the earth's atmosphere. *The ozone layer is slowly being destroyed by man-made chemicals.*

**aerate** (er´ āt´) expose to and mix with air. *The water in our swimming pool is aerated.*

**bract** (brakt) a small leaf growing at the base of a flower or on a flower stalk. *She accidentally broke the bract on the flower.*

Name: _____ Date: _____

# Unit 6: Ecology: *Skills and Practice*

**Directions:** Write a **synonym** from the list of vocabulary words below on the line. A **synonym** is a word that means the same or nearly the same.

| noxious | woodland | conservation | camouflage |
|---------|----------|--------------|------------|
| temperate | grassland | endangered | bivouac |

1. disguise _____

2. poisonous _____

3. camp _____

4. jeopardy _____

5. mild _____

6. forest _____

7. savanna _____

8. preservation _____

**Did You Know?** Julius Sterling Morton was responsible for establishing the first Arbor Day in the United States. Arbor Day is a day set aside for planting trees.

**Directions:** Fill in each blank with the correct vocabulary word from below.

| dust bowl | ozone layer | deciduous | coniferous |
|-----------|-------------|-----------|------------|
| deforestation | species | | |

1. pines _____

2. shield of air _____

3. western plains _____

4. maples, elms _____

5. animals _____

6. tree removal _____

**Directions:** Write a sentence for each of the vocabulary words below on your own paper. Remember to check for spelling and punctuation.

| biome | ecosystem | tundra | broad-leaved | bract |
|-------|-----------|--------|--------------|-------|
| humus | mammalogy | canopy | understory | aerate |

### Extend Your Vocabulary

1. Make a list of ways you can recycle.
2. Research the food chain and make a drawing of a food chain you are a part of.
3. Choose an endangered species. Write a report.
4. Read as a class, *50 Simple Things Kids Can Do to Save the Earth*. Write a reaction.

Name: _____ Date: _____

# Unit 6: Ecology: *Vocabulary Quiz*

**Directions:** Match each vocabulary word with the correct meaning. Write the word on the line next to the meaning.

| biome | ecosystem | coniferous | deciduous | humus |
|-------|-----------|------------|-----------|-------|
| savanna | grassland | tundra | temperate | bract |
| woodland | broad-leaved | mammalogy | conservation | ozone layer |
| endangered | dust bowl | species | deforestation | canopy |
| camouflage | understory | noxious | bivouac | aerate |

1. _____ layer that consists of the tops of smaller trees, which receives less light than the canopy

2. _____ a grassy plain with few or no trees

3. _____ area in the western plains of the United States and Canada where dust storms are frequent and violent

4. _____ having broad leaves; leaves that are not needles

5. _____ green and leafy layer in the rain forest 80–150 feet above the ground, where large, broad leaves catch and block both rain and sunlight

6. _____ a large geographical area having generally the same climate and vegetation

7. _____ very harmful; poisonous

8. _____ branch of zoology dealing with mammals

9. _____ a small leaf growing at the base of a flower or flower stalk

10. _____ shedding leaves each year

11. _____ brought into danger or peril

12. _____ a community of interlocking parts that act upon each other in life's grand plan

13. _____ a disguise or false appearance for the purpose of concealing

14. _____ a dark-brown or black part of soil formed from decayed leaves and other vegetable matter

15. _____ a protective shield of air high up in the earth's atmosphere

16. _____ a preserving from harm or decay; protection from loss

17. _____ groups of animals or plants that have certain permanent characteristics in common and are able to interbreed

18. _____ bearing cones

19. _____ removal of trees

20. _____ land covered with trees

21. _____ camp outdoors, usually without tents or with very small tents

22. _____ land with grass on it, used for pasture

23. _____ expose to and mix with air

24. _____ not very hot and not very cold

25. _____ a vast, level, treeless plain in the arctic regions

# Unit 7: Space

Rockets have made space exploration possible. They are the only vehicles powerful enough to carry spacecraft away from the surface of the earth. Rockets began carrying satellites into orbit in 1957. In 1961, the first man was sent into space by the USSR. By 1969, the United States had landed the first men on the moon. Today, the biggest problem facing the future of space exploration is cost, not technology.

eclipse (i klips′)

lunar (lōō′ nər)

constellation (kon′ stə lā′ shən)

celestial (sə les′ chəl)

interplanetary (in′ tər plan′ ə ter′ ē)

asteroid (as′ tər oid′)

astronomy (ə stron′ ə mē)

cosmos (koz′ mōs′)

ever-expanding (ev′ ər ek spand′ ing)

planetarium (plan′ i ter′ ē əm)

sunspot (sun′ spot′)

black hole (blak hōl)

astronomer (ə stron′ ə mər)

aurora (ô rôr′ ə)

satellite (sat′ ′l īt′)

orbit (ôr′ bit)

corona (kə rō′ nə)

gravity (grav′ i tē)

supernova (sōō′ pər nō′ və)

nebula (neb′ yə lə)

galaxy (gal′ ək sē)

quasars (kwā′ särz′)

solstice (sōl′ stis)

comet (kom′ it)

equinox (ē′ kwi noks′)

# Unit 7: Space: *Get the Facts!*

**eclipse** (i klips´) a complete or partial blocking of light passing from one heavenly body to another. *There can be a solar eclipse or a lunar eclipse.*

**lunar** (loo´ nər) of the moon; like the moon. *A lunar month is the period of one complete revolution of the moon around the earth.*

**constellation** (kon´ stə lā´ shən) group of stars usually having a recognized shape. *Last night I observed constellations in the sky.*

**celestial** (sə les´ chəl) of the sky or the heavens. *The stars are celestial bodies.*

**interplanetary** (in´ tər plan´ ə ter´ ē) situated or taking place between planets. *Will there ever be interplanetary travel?*

**asteroid** (as´ tər oid´) any of the thousands of very small planets that revolve about the sun; planetoid. *The asteroids revolve around the sun in a wide band between Mars and Jupiter.*

**astronomy** (ə stron´ ə mē) science that deals with the sun, moon, planets, stars, and other heavenly bodies. *He is taking a course called astronomy at his college.*

**cosmos** (koz´ mōs´) the universe as thought of as an orderly, harmonious system. *Can the cosmos get larger?*

**ever-expanding** (ev´ ər ek spand´ ing) increasing or growing larger indefinitely. *The universe is ever-expanding.*

**planetarium** (plan´ i ter´ ē əm) building that has an apparatus that shows the movement of the sun, moon, planets, and stars by projecting lights onto the inside of a dome. *I saw a great star presentation at the planetarium.*

**sunspot** (sun´ spot´) one of the dark spots that appears from time to time on the surface of the sun. *The sunspots are much cooler than the other parts of the sun.*

**black hole** (blak hōl) an invisible object in space with mass and gravitational force that is so strong that even light is unable to escape from it. *What part does a supernova play in creating a black hole?*

**astronomer** (ə stron´ ə mər) one who is skilled in astronomy or who makes observations of celestial bodies. *The astronomer used a high-powered telescope to observe the stars.*

**aurora** (ô rôr´ ə) the display of lights in the near polar latitudes. *Auroras can be seen in Alaska.*

**satellite** (sat´ ´l it´) an artificial object launched by a rocket into an orbit around the earth or heavenly body. *The* Sputnik *was the first satellite launched into space.*

**orbit** (ôr´ bit) curved, usually somewhat oval path of a heavenly body, planet, or satellite about another body in space. *The earth's orbit is around the sun.*

**corona** (kə rō´ nə) a crown of glowing gases seen around the sun. *The corona can be seen during a total solar eclipse.*

**gravity** (grav´ i tē) the natural force that causes objects to move or tend to move toward the center of the earth. *Earth's gravity holds us in place on the planet.*

**supernova** (soo´ pər nō´ və) the explosion of a star. *Is a telescope necessary to see a supernova?*

**nebula** (neb´ yə lə) cloud of gas and dust in space. *Within the nebula, a star is created.*

**galaxy** (gal´ ək sē) a system of billions of stars, gases, and dust. *The sun and earth belong to the same galaxy.*

**quasars** (kwā´ särz´) very bright objects in space that may be the powerhouses of developing galaxies. *Quasars may be ten billion light years away from us.*

**solstice** (sōl´ stis) a point in Earth's orbit around the sun where daylight is either the longest or shortest amount possible. *The summer solstice is on either June 21 or 22.*

**comet** (kom´ it) a small, frozen mass of dust and gas revolving around the sun; it appears as a bright heavenly body with a starlike center and often with a cloudy tail of light. *Comets move around the sun.*

**equinox** (ē´ kwi noks´) a point in Earth's orbit around the sun where nights and days are the same length. *The first day of autumn begins on the equinox.*

Name: _____  Date: _____

# Unit 7: Space: *Skills and Practice*

**Directions:** Categorize each of the vocabulary words below and write the word on the line under the correct category. Some words may be used more than once.

| | | | | |
|---|---|---|---|---|
| sunspot | lunar | galaxy | interplanetary | corona |
| nebula | orbit | equinox | constellation | eclipse |
| solstice | asteroid | supernova | | |

**Stars**

_____

_____

_____

_____

**Sun**

_____

_____

_____

_____

**Planets**

_____

_____

_____

**Moon**

_____

_____

**Did You Know?** The record for the longest comet tail was the Great Comet of 1843. Its tail stretched 200 million miles!

**Directions:** Write a sentence for the following words on your own paper. Remember to check your spelling and punctuation.

| | | | | |
|---|---|---|---|---|
| celestial | astronomy | cosmos | galaxy | ever-expanding |
| planetarium | black hole | astronomer | gravity | satellite |

## Extend Your Vocabulary

1. Research the order of the planets and illustrate them in a diagram. Label the planets.
2. Pick a planet and write a report on it.
3. Make a list of celestial bodies.
4. Write a report about a planetarium and include the things you do there. Visit one if possible.

Name: _____   Date: _____

# Unit 7: Space: *Vocabulary Quiz*

**Directions:** Match each vocabulary word with the correct meaning. Write the word on the line next to the meaning.

| | | | | |
|---|---|---|---|---|
| eclipse | lunar | constellation | celestial | interplanetary |
| asteroid | cosmos | astronomy | sunspot | ever-expanding |
| equinox | comet | planetarium | black hole | astronomer |
| aurora | satellite | orbit | corona | gravity |
| nebula | supernova | galaxy | quasars | solstice |

1. _____ curved, usually somewhat oval path of a heavenly body, planet, or satellite about another body in space

2. _____ of the moon, like the moon

3. _____ one who is skilled in astronomy

4. _____ any of thousands of very small planets that revolve about the sun; planetoid

5. _____ the natural force that causes objects to move or tend to move toward the center of the earth

6. _____ increasing or growing larger indefinitely

7. _____ a point in Earth's orbit around the sun where daylight is either the longest or shortest amount possible

8. _____ an invisible object in space with mass and gravitational force that is so strong that even light is unable to escape from it

9. _____ a crown of glowing gases seen around the sun

10. _____ of the sky or the heavens

11. _____ the display of lights in the near polar latitudes

12. _____ a complete or partial blocking of light passing from one heavenly body to another

13. _____ cloud of gas and dust in space

14. _____ science that deals with the sun, moon, planets, stars, and other heavenly bodies

15. _____ one of the dark spots that appears on the surface of the sun

16. _____ a point in Earth's orbit around the sun where nights and days are the same length

17. _____ building that has an apparatus that shows the movement of the sun, moon, planets, and stars by projecting lights onto the inside of a dome

18. _____ the explosion of a star

19. _____ the universe as thought of as an orderly, harmonious system

20. _____ an artificial object launched by rockets into an orbit around the earth or a heavenly body

21. _____ group of stars usually having a recognized shape

22. _____ a system of billions of stars, gases, and dust

23. _____ situated or taking place between planets

24. _____ very bright objects in space that may be the powerhouses of developing galaxies

25. _____ a small, frozen mass of dust and gas revolving around the sun

# Unit 8: Immigration

America has a history of immigration. A number of varied groups have immigrated to America. They include the earliest Native Americans, Pilgrims, African slaves, Eastern and Western Europeans, Asians, and people from North and South American countries. The immigrants brought their own customs and traditions that have become an integral part of America.

swindler (swind´ lər)

steerage (stir´ ij)

surname (sûr´ nām´)

naturalization (nach´ ər əl i zā´ shən)

ethnic (eth´ nik)

famine (fam´ ən)

heritage (her´ i tij´)

wayworn (wā´ wôrn´)

stowage (stō´ ij)

manifest (man´ ə fest´)

chopsticks (chop´ stiks´)

realize (rē´ ə līz´)

lure (lo͝or)

indentured (in den´ chərd)

melting pot (melt´ ing pot)

patronymic (pa´ trō nim´ ik)

fiesta (fē es´ tə)

persecuted (pûr´ sə kyo͞ot´ əd)

slang (slang)

homeland (hōm´ land´)

custom (kus´ təm)

moor (mo͝or)

bilingual (bī ling´ gwəl)

treasured (trezh´ ərd)

choice (chois)

29

# Unit 8: Immigration: *Get the Facts!*

**swindler** (swind´ lər) person who cheats or defrauds. *The new immigrants were susceptible to swindlers.*

**indentured** (in den´ chərd) bound by a contract to serve someone else. *Some people who came to America were indentured for several years.*

**steerage** (stir´ ij) the part of a passenger ship occupied by passengers traveling at the cheapest rate. *The immigrants traveled in the steerage of the ship.*

**melting pot** (melt´ ing pot) a place exhibiting racial uniting and absorbing into the cultural traditions of a group or population. *The United States is a melting pot of many nationalities.*

**surname** (sûr´ nām´) the last name; family name. *Many immigrants Americanized their surnames.*

**patronymic** (pa´ trō nim´ ik) derived from the name of the father or a paternal ancestor, usually by the addition of an affix. *The names Johnson and Ivanovich both have patronymic suffixes that make the name mean "son of John."*

**naturalization** (nach´ ər əl i zā´ shən) a foreigner being admitted to citizenship. *Naturalization is a goal of many immigrants.*

**fiesta** (fē es´ tə) festivity; festival. *The people arriving from Mexico brought their tradition of celebrating holidays with fiestas.*

**ethnic** (eth´ nik) of people of foreign birth or descent. *There are many ethnic groups in the United States.*

**persecuted** (pûr´ sə kyoōt´ əd) treated badly; harmed again and again; oppressed. *The Jewish people were persecuted because of their race and beliefs.*

**famine** (fam´ ən) lack of food in a place; a time of starving. *Famine was one of the reasons why people immigrated to America.*

**slang** (slang) words, phrases, or meanings not accepted as proper English. *Slang in our English language has caused misunderstandings with immigrants.*

**heritage** (her´ i tij´) what is handed down from one generation to the next; inheritance. *He handed down his Russian heritage with some of its tradition to his son.*

**homeland** (hōm´ land´) country that is one's home; one's native land. *The Polish immigrant missed her homeland.*

**wayworn** (wā´ wôrn´) wearied by traveling. *The wayworn immigrant was exhausted after the long, hard journey.*

**custom** (kus´ təm) any usual action or practice; habit; a long-established habit having the force of law. *Was that a custom in your country?*

**stowage** (stō´ ij) a place or receptacle for storage; storage. *The boy was found in the stowage of the boat.*

**moor** (moŏr) fix firmly; secure; tie down or anchor a ship. *The ship was moored at the dock.*

**manifest** (man´ ə fest´) an itemized list of cargo or passengers on a ship. *My German grandmother's name was on the ship's manifest.*

**bilingual** (bī ling´ gwəl) able to speak another language as well as one's own; knowing two languages. *The little girl is bilingual.*

**chopsticks** (chop´ stiks´) pair of small, slender sticks used by the Chinese and Japanese to raise food to the mouth. *The Chinese boy eats with chopsticks.*

**treasured** (trezh´ ərd) valuable; much loved or valued. *Immigrants could only bring a few of their treasured possessions with them on the ship when they left their countries.*

**realize** (rē´ ə līz´) to make real; achieve; be fully aware of. *Some immigrants were able to realize their dreams in the United States.*

**choice** (chois) act of picking out; selecting from a number of items. *The immigrants had freedom of choice in the United States.*

**lure** (loŏr) power of attracting or fascinating; charm; attraction. *It was the lure of opportunities that brought immigrants to the United States.*

Name: _____        Date: _____

# Unit 8: Immigration: *Skills and Practice*

**Directions:** Write a **synonym** from the list of vocabulary words below on the line next to each word. A **synonym** is a word that means the same or nearly the same.

| heritage | moor | swindler | persecuted | fiesta |
|----------|------|----------|------------|--------|
| custom | treasured | stowage | famine | |

1. hunger _____    2. cheater _____

3. valued _____    4. festival _____

5. secure _____    6. storage _____

7. oppressed _____   8. inheritance _____

9. habit _____

**Did You Know?** Immigrants brought musical traditions from their homelands. The opera came from Italy; symphonies came from Russia; and calypso came from the Caribbean.

**Directions:** Write an **antonym** from the list of vocabulary words below on the line next to each word. An **antonym** is a word that means the opposite or nearly opposite.

| wayworn | lure | slang | realize | choice |
|---------|------|-------|---------|--------|

1. misunderstood _____   2. repel _____

3. active _____      4. mandate _____

5. formal _____

**Directions:** Write a sentence for the following words on your own paper. Remember to check your spelling and punctuation.

| manifest | bilingual | chopsticks | indentured | steerage |
|----------|-----------|------------|------------|----------|
| melting pot | surname | patronymic | naturalization | ethnic |
| homeland | | | | |

## Extend Your Vocabulary

1. Pretend you're an immigrant child. Write a diary entry of a day on the ship. How did you feel?
2. Make a list of things you treasure.
3. Read the book *If Your Name Was Changed at Ellis Island*. Write a reaction.
4. Research different groups of immigrants who came to the United States and make a time line of the different groups' arrivals.

Name: _____    Date: _____

# Unit 8: Immigration: *Vocabulary Quiz*

**Directions:** Match each vocabulary word with the correct meaning. Write the word on the line next to the meaning.

| | | | | |
|---|---|---|---|---|
| **swindler** | **indentured** | **steerage** | **melting pot** | **surname** |
| **patronymic** | **naturalization** | **fiesta** | **persecuted** | **ethnic** |
| **famine** | **treasured** | **slang** | **heritage** | **homeland** |
| **custom** | **stowage** | **moor** | **manifest** | **bilingual** |
| **chopsticks** | **realize** | **choice** | **lure** | **wayworn** |

1. _____ wearied by traveling

2. _____ a place exhibiting racial uniting and absorbing into the cultural tradition of a group or population

3. _____ able to speak another language as well as one's own; knowing two languages

4. _____ what is handed down from one generation to the next; inheritance

5. _____ pair of small, slender sticks used by the Chinese and Japanese to raise food to the mouth

6. _____ bound by a contract to serve someone else

7. _____ any usual action or practice; habit; a long-established habit having the force of law

8. _____ foreigner being admitted to citizenship

9. _____ country that is one's home

10. _____ of people of foreign birth or descent

11. _____ fix firmly; secure; tie down or anchor a ship

12. _____ person who cheats or defrauds

13. _____ valuable; much loved or valued

14. _____ last name; family name

15. _____ act of picking out; selecting from a number of items

16. _____ treated badly; harmed again and again; oppressed

17. _____ place or receptacle for storage; storage

18. _____ the part of a passenger ship occupied by passengers traveling at the cheapest rate

19. _____ to make real; achieve; be fully aware of

20. _____ derived from the name of the father or a paternal ancestor

21. _____ power of attracting or fascinating; charm; attraction

22. _____ lack of food in a place; a time of starving

23. _____ an itemized list of cargo or passengers on a ship

24. _____ festivity; festival

25. _____ words, phrases, or meanings, etc., not accepted as proper English

# Unit 9: Ancient Civilizations

Early civilizations included Egypt, ancient China, ancient India, and Mesopotamia. Rivers were a key to the survival and growth of these civilizations. Around the four river valleys farmers lived and built the first cities and kingdoms. Even though people began to move into these lands at about the same time, each civilization developed in different ways with its own special culture.

| | |
|---|---|
| scribe (skrīb) | papyrus (pə pī´ rəs) |
| hieroglyphics (hī rō´ glif´ iks) | pyramid (pir´ ə mid) |
| pharaoh (far´ ō) | ankh (ängk) |
| ibis (ī´ bis) | ziggurat (zig´ o͝o rat´) |
| cuneiform (kū nē´ ə fôrm´) | Judaism (jo͞o´ dē iz´ əm) |
| polytheism (pol´ i thē iz´ əm) | monotheism (mon´ ə thē iz´ əm) |
| subcontinent (sub´ kont´ ’nənt) | citadel (sit´ ə del´) |
| dynasty (dī´ nəs tē) | oracle (or´ ə kəl) |
| flourish (flûr´ ish) | Hebrew (hē´ bro͞o) |
| proverb (prov´ ûrb´) | irrigation (ir´ i gā´ shən) |
| silt (silt) | charioteer (char´ ē ə tir´) |
| empire (em´ pīr´) | migration (mī grā´ shən) |
| tributary (trib´ ū ter´ ē) | |

# Unit 9: Ancient Civilizations: *Get the Facts!*

**scribe** (skrīb) person who copies manuscripts. *Before printing was invented, there were many scribes.*

**papyrus** (pə pī´ rəs) a type of paper made from reeds. *Papyrus was used by ancient Egyptians for writing and keeping records.*

**hieroglyphics** (hī rō´ glif´ iks) a system of writing in ancient Egypt. *Hieroglyphics used pictures and signs to stand for objects, sounds, and ideas.*

**pyramid** (pir´ ə mid) huge stone structure built by the ancient Egyptians as a royal tomb. *The pyramids had a square base and four triangular sides.*

**pharaoh** (far´ ō) the supreme ruler of Egypt. *In ancient Egypt, a pharaoh was worshipped as a god.*

**ankh** (ängk) an ancient Egyptian symbol of life, a cross with a top loop. *The pharaoh was often pictured holding an ankh.*

**ibis** (ī´ bis) a large, long-legged wading bird of warm regions, having a long, downward-curving bill. *The ancient Egyptians regarded the ibis as sacred.*

**ziggurat** (zig´ ŏŏ rat´) large temple built by ancient Sumerians to worship their gods and goddesses. *The ziggurats were the tallest buildings, which made them nearer to the gods.*

**cuneiform** (kū nē´ ə fòrm´) system of writing developed in ancient Sumeria. *Cuneiform used wedge-shaped symbols.*

**Judaism** (jōō´ dē iz´ əm) a world religion founded by the ancient Hebrews. *Judaism is followed today by more than 17 million people, known as Jews.*

**polytheism** (pol´ i thē iz´ əm) belief in many gods. *The Egyptians believed in polytheism.*

**monotheism** (mon´ ə thē iz´ əm) belief in one god. *The Hebrews practiced monotheism.*

**subcontinent** (sub´ kont´ ’nənt) large land mass that is connected to a continent. *The Indian peninsula is a subcontinent.*

**citadel** (sit´ ə del´) walled-in area, similar to a fortress, that was built to protect a city. *People go to a citadel for protection from invaders.*

**dynasty** (dī´ nəs tē) line of rulers who belong to the same family and pass control from one generation to the next. *The Shang Dynasty lasted 600 years.*

**oracle** (or´ ə kəl) a special priest in ancient Chinese society who was believed to receive messages from the gods. *The king went to the oracle for help.*

**flourish** (flûr´ ish) grow or develop with vigor; do well; thrive. *Civilization flourished in the Indus River Valley.*

**Hebrew** (hē´ brōō) Jew; Israelite. *The Bible tells us that the earliest Hebrews were shepherds who lived in Mesopotamia.*

**proverb** (prov´ ûrb´) a short, wise saying used for a long time by many people. *Proverbs are short sayings used to pass along ideas quickly.*

**irrigation** (ir´ i gā´ shən) the watering of dry land by means of streams, canals, or pipes in order to grow more crops. *Irrigation helps farmers grow more crops.*

**silt** (silt) bits of black soil, sand, and clay laid down by flowing water. *The Nile flood waters carried silt.*

**charioteer** (char´ ē ə tir´) person who drives a chariot. *He was a famous Roman charioteer.*

**empire** (em´ pīr´) a group of lands and people under one government. *Trade was extensive throughout the Egyptian Empire.*

**migration** (mī grā´ shən) the movement of a large group of people from one country or region to another in order to settle there. *An ancient Indian legend tells of a great migration.*

**tributary** (trib´ ū ter´ ē) a small river or stream that flows into a large river. *Many villages were built along tributaries.*

34

Name: _____     Date: _____

# Unit 9: Ancient Civilizations: *Skills and Practice*

**Directions:** For each word give a **synonym** from the vocabulary word list below. A **synonym** is a word that means the same or nearly the same.

| proverb | pharaoh | citadel | tributary |
| scribe | ziggurat | Hebrew | oracle |

1. fortress _____
3. stream _____
5. priest _____
7. writer _____

2. temple _____
4. Jew _____
6. adage _____
8. Egyptian ruler _____

**Did You Know?** There were approximately 50 million people in the Roman Empire; it covered countries from Britain to Africa. Because of this, the empire had different climates. The Romans suffered from the extremely hot summer temperatures in Egypt, while others shivered in the Swiss Alps and Northern Britain.

**Directions:** Write an **antonym** from the list of vocabulary words below on the line next to each word. An **antonym** is a word that means the opposite or nearly opposiite.

| migration | flourish | irrigation | monotheism |

1. polytheism _____
3. drought _____

2. wither _____
4. stability _____

**Directions:** Write a sentence for the following words on your own paper. Remember to check your spelling and punctuation.

| papyrus | hieroglyphics | pyramid | ibis | cuneiform |
| Judaism | subcontinent | dynasty | silt | ankh |
| charioteer | | | | |

## Extend Your Vocabulary

1. Find a website on the Internet on hieroglyphics. Print out your name in hieroglyphics.
2. Research a pyramid. Divide the class into three groups. Make pyramids out of three different types of material.
3. Find three proverbs and write them on a sheet of paper. Explain what they actually mean.
4. Research King Tutankhamun. Write a persuasive piece about his death: murder or not?

Name: _____     Date: _____

# Unit 9: Ancient Civilizations: *Vocabulary Quiz*

**Directions:** Match each vocabulary word with the correct meaning. Write the word on the line next to the meaning.

| | | | | |
|---|---|---|---|---|
| **scribe** | **papyrus** | **hieroglyphics** | **pyramid** | **pharaoh** |
| **ankh** | **ibis** | **ziggurat** | **cuneiform** | **Judaism** |
| **polytheism** | **monotheism** | **subcontinent** | **citadel** | **dynasty** |
| **oracle** | **flourish** | **Hebrew** | **proverb** | **irrigation** |
| **silt** | **charioteer** | **empire** | **migration** | **tributary** |

1. _____ a line of rulers who belong to the same family and pass control from one generation to the next

2. _____ huge stone structure built by the ancient Egyptians as a royal tomb

3. _____ the watering of dry land by means of streams, canals, or pipes in order to grow more crops

4. _____ a large temple built by ancient Sumerians

5. _____ a special priest in ancient Chinese society who was believed to receive messages from the gods

6. _____ person who copies manuscripts

7. _____ bits of black soil, sand, and clay laid down by flowing water

8. _____ a world religion founded by the ancient Hebrews

9. _____ the movement of a large group of people from one country or region to another in order to settle there

10. _____ an ancient Egyptian symbol of life, a cross with a loop on top

11. _____ a walled-in area, similar to a fortress, built to protect a city

12. _____ a system of writing in ancient Egypt

13. _____ Jew; Israelite

14. _____ a system of writing developed in ancient Sumeria

15. _____ person who drives a chariot

16. _____ belief in one god

17. _____ a group of lands and people under one government

18. _____ a large, long-legged wading bird of warm regions, having a long, downward-curving bill

19. _____ grow or develop with vigor; do well; thrive

20. _____ the supreme ruler of ancient Egypt

21. _____ a short, wise saying used for a long time by many people

22. _____ a type of paper made from reeds

23. _____ a large land mass that is connected to a continent

24. _____ a small river or stream that flows into a large river

25. _____ belief in many gods

# Unit 10: Wishes and Dreams

We often wish we had things that we do not possess or dream of being someone else or somewhere else. Wishing and dreaming help us to accomplish and reach our goals and ambitions. Sometimes wishing can come from desiring or longing for loved ones we miss and would like to see again. There are some people who claim they can analyze and interpret dreams.

anticipate (an tis´ ə pāt´)

covet (kuv´ it)

inclination (in´ klə nā´ shən)

wistful (wist´ fəl)

yearn (yûrn)

cherish (cher´ ish)

intention (in ten´ shən)

imagery (im´ ij rē)

ponder (pon´ dər)

expectation (ek´ spek tā´ shən)

delusion (di lōō´ zhən)

visionary (vizh´ ə ner´ ē)

whimsy (hwim´ zē)

aspire (ə spīr´)

enviable (en´ vē ə bəl)

desire (di zīr´)

ambition (am bish´ ən)

mirage (mi räzh´)

inspiration (in´ spə rā´ shən)

hankering (hang´ kər ing)

illusion (i lōō´ zhən)

abstract (ab´ strakt´)

trance (trans)

figment (fig´ mənt)

idealize (ī dē´ ə līz´)

# Unit 10: Wishes and Dreams: *Get the Facts!*

**anticipate** (an tis´ə pāt´) look forward to; expect. *We anticipate a great Christmas Day.*

**aspire** (ə spīr´) have an ambition for something; desire earnestly. *She aspires to be the next beauty queen.*

**covet** (kuv´ it) desire something that belongs to another. *Daniel coveted Jake's new bike.*

**enviable** (en´ vē ə bəl) to be envied; worth having. *Stan has an enviable school report card.*

**inclination** (in´ klə nā´ shən) preference; liking. *The twins had a strong inclination towards gymnastics.*

**desire** (di zīr´) a wanting or longing; strong wish. *She had a desire to be first in her class.*

**wistful** (wist´ fəl) longing; yearning. *Ted looked with wistful eyes at the new golf clubs.*

**ambition** (am bish´ ən) a strong desire for fame, honor, or wealth. *His ambition helped him earn the job of his dreams.*

**yearn** (yûrn) feel a longing or desire. *She yearned for home after the week-long camp.*

**mirage** (mi räzh´) an optical illusion, usually in the desert, at sea, or on a paved road. *The lost and thirsty man saw a mirage of water in the desert.*

**cherish** (cher´ ish) hold dear; treat with affection. *Parents cherish their children and wish only the best for them.*

**inspiration** (in´ spə rā´ shən) influence of thought and strong feelings on actions. *She got inspiration from watching the professional dancers.*

**intention** (in ten´ shən) purpose; design; plan. *Your intentions for a new homeless shelter are good.*

**hankering** (hang´ kər ing) have a longing or craving. *I had a hankering for a piece of chocolate.*

**imagery** (im´ ij rē) pictures formed in the mind. *My best dream contained vivid imagery.*

**illusion** (i lōō´ zhən) appearance or feeling that misleads because it is not real. *The lighted picture gave the illusion of moving water.*

**ponder** (pon´ dər) consider carefully; think over. *He was pondering which vacation to take.*

**abstract** (ab´ strakt´) thought apart from any particular object or real thing. *The dream was too abstract to remember.*

**expectation** (ek´ spek tā´ shən) anticipation; something expected. *He had expectations of getting an 'A' on the test.*

**trance** (trans) state of unconsciousness, somewhat like sleep. *She sat in a trance as she thought about her evening.*

**delusion** (di lōō´ zhən) a false belief or opinion. *He was under the delusion that the ride would be free.*

**figment** (fig´ mənt) something imagined; made-up story. *The big purple monster was a figment of the child's imagination.*

**visionary** (vizh´ ə ner´ ē) person whose ideas seem impractical; dreamer. *The visionary child daydreams often.*

**idealize** (ī dē´ ə līz´) think of or represent as perfect rather than as is actually true. *The boys idealized the professional soccer player.*

**whimsy** (hwim´ zē) an odd or fanciful notion. *Some children's programs are full of whimsy.*

38

Name: _____     Date: _____

# Unit 10: Wishes and Dreams: *Skills and Practice*

**Directions:** Write a **synonym** from the list of vocabulary words below on the line next to each word. A **synonym** is a word that means the same or nearly the same.

| | | | | |
|---|---|---|---|---|
| desire | mirage | enviable | wistful | inclination |
| ambition | yearn | hankering | trance | anticipate |
| intention | visionary | ponder | abstract | |

1. illusion _____     2. preference _____

3. craving _____     4. expect _____

5. dreamer _____     6. consider _____

7. purpose _____     8. unconsciousness _____

9. unreal _____     10. goal _____

11. longing _____  _____  _____

12. worthy _____

**Did You Know?** The origin of dream interpretation is unknown. Some of the earliest examples of dreams being interpreted were in the Bible.

**Directions:** Write a sentence for the following words on your own paper. Remember to check your spelling and punctuation.

| | | | | |
|---|---|---|---|---|
| aspire | covet | cherish | inspiration | imagery | expectation |
| delusion | whimsy | figment | idealize | |

**Extend Your Vocabulary**

1. Write about one of your dreams. Try to explain what it means.
2. If you had three wishes, what would they be and why? Write about it.
3. Make a list of visionaries in the history of the United States.
4. What are some things you have a hankering for? Compare your list with a classmate's.

Name: _____   Date: _____

# Unit 10: Wishes and Dreams: *Vocabulary Quiz*

**Directions:** Match each vocabulary word with the correct meaning. Write the word on the line next to the meaning.

| anticipate | aspire | covet | enviable | inclination |
|---|---|---|---|---|
| desire | wistful | yearn | ambition | inspiration |
| mirage | cherish | ponder | intention | hankering |
| imagery | illusion | abstract | expectation | delusion |
| figment | visionary | idealize | whimsy | trance |

1. _____ appearance or feeling that misleads because it is not real

2. _____ look forward to; expect

3. _____ anticipation; something expected

4. _____ to be envied; worth having

5. _____ something imagined; made-up story

6. _____ hold dear; treat with affection

7. _____ consider carefully; think over

8. _____ have an ambition for something

9. _____ a false belief or opinion

10. _____ longing; yearning

11. _____ thought of apart from any particular object or real thing

12. _____ preference; liking

13. _____ person whose ideas seem impractical; dreamer

14. _____ purpose; design; plan

15. _____ an odd or fanciful notion

16. _____ a wanting or longing; strong wish

17. _____ state of unconsciousness somewhat like sleep

18. _____ a strong desire for fame, honor, or wealth

19. _____ think of or represent as perfect rather than as is actually true

20. _____ pictures formed in the mind

21. _____ desire something that belongs to another

22. _____ feel a longing or desire

23. _____ influence of thought and strong feelings on actions

24. _____ an optical illusion, usually in the desert, at sea, or on a paved road

25. _____ have a longing or craving

# Unit 11: Archaeology

Archaeology is the scientific study of the people, customs, and life of ancient times. Since there are few or possibly no written records, archaeologists need to study weapons, tools, pottery, or any objects they can find to tell about the people of those times. Archaeologists need to dig into the earth to find these objects. It takes time, patience, and teamwork.

excavation (ek´ skə vā´ shən)

prehistoric (prē´ hi stôr´ ik)

lithics (lith´ iks)

archive (är´ kiv´)

mosaic (mō zā´ ik)

exhume (eks hyo͞om´)

dating (dā´ ting)

architectural (är´ ki tek´ chər əl)

tedious (tē´ dē əs)

sedimentary (sed´ ə men´ tə rē)

gemstone (jem´ stōn´)

ammonite (am´ ə nīt´)

relic (rel´ ik)

archaeologist (är´ kē ol´ ə jist)

artifact (är´ tə fakt´)

anthropology (an´ thrə pol´ ə jē)

researcher (ri sûr´ chər)

shard (shärd)

perseverance (pûr´ sə vir´ əns)

expedition (ek´ spi dish´ ən)

amber (am´ bər)

igneous (ig´ nē əs)

metamorphic (met´ ə môr´ fik)

paleontologist (pā´ lē on tol´ ə jist)

historian (hi stôr´ ē ən)

# Unit 11: Archaeology: *Get the Facts!*

**excavation** (ek´ skə vā´ shən) a digging out; making hollow; hollowing out. *The excavation turned up many artifacts.*

**archaeologist** (är´ kē ol´ ə jist) an expert in archaeology, the study of the people, customs, and life of ancient times. *An archaeologist studies objects to find out how people lived many years ago.*

**prehistoric** (prē´ hi stôr´ ik) of or belonging to time before histories were written. *They found some prehistoric tools at the archaeological digging site.*

**artifact** (är´ tə fakt´) anything made by human skill or work, especially tools or weapons. *The archaeologist studied the artifacts of an ancient Roman village.*

**lithics** (lith´ iks) stone tools. *The diggers found some lithics at the archaeological site.*

**anthropology** (an´ thrə pol´ ə jē) the science dealing with the origin, development, races, and customs of human beings. *He is studying anthropology at the university.*

**archive** (är´ kīv´) place where public records or historical documents are kept. *The woman had to go to the archives to research the historic information.*

**researcher** (ri sûr´ chər) person who does research; investigator. *The researcher made a great discovery.*

**mosaic** (mō zā´ ik) decorative design of small pieces of stone, glass, tile, or wood of different colors inlaid to form a design or picture. *He found ancient mosaics at the site.*

**shard** (shärd) broken pottery. *He studied some shards at the dig site.*

**exhume** (eks hyōōm´) to dig out of the earth. *The archaeologist exhumed the artifacts from the tomb.*

**perseverance** (pûr´ sə vîr´ əns) a sticking to a purpose or an aim; never giving up what one has set out to do. *Digging out a fossil takes perseverance.*

**dating** (dā´ ting) to mark with characteristics typical of a particular period; to show the age of. *Dating rocks from fossils can be done by scientists.*

**expedition** (ek´ spi dish´ ən) journey for some special purpose. *They went on an expedition to study the ruins.*

**architectural** (är´ ki tek´ chər əl) of the art of planning and designing buildings. *We studied the architectural designs of the Greek buildings.*

**amber** (am´ bər) a hard, yellow or yellowish-brown gum; resin. *Some prehistoric insects have been found in hardened amber.*

**tedious** (tē´ dē əs) long and tiring. *Digging at a site can be tedious.*

**igneous** (ig´ nē əs) rock formed by the cooling of melted rock material either within or on the surface of the earth. *Basalt is an igneous rock.*

**sedimentary** (sed´ ə men´ tə rē) rock formed by the depositing of sediment. *Sandstone is a sedimentary rock.*

**metamorphic** (met´ ə môr´ fik) rock changed in structure by heat, moisture, and pressure. *Marble is a metamorphic rock.*

**gemstone** (jem´ stōn´) a precious or semi-precious stone, especially when cut and polished for ornamentation; jewel. *A ruby is a gemstone.*

**paleontologist** (pā´ lē on tol´ ə jist) an expert in the science of the forms of life existing in prehistoric time, such as fossil animals and plants. *The paleontologist was studying land fossils.*

**ammonite** (am´ ə nīt´) coiled, flat, chambered fossil shell of an extinct mollusk. *There are many fossilized ammonites that are found by archaeologists.*

**historian** (hi stôr´ ē ən) person who writes about history; expert in history. *She is an excellent historian in Roman history.*

**relic** (rel´ ik) an item left from the past. *He found a relic among the Greek ruins.*

Name: _____     Date: _____

# Unit 11: Archaeology: *Skills and Practice*

**Directions:** For each word give a **synonym** from the vocabulary word list below. A **synonym** is a word that means the same or nearly the same.

|  |  |  |  |  |
|---|---|---|---|---|
| **lithics** | **amber** | **artifact** | **gemstone** | **expedition** |
| **archive** | **mosaic** | **researcher** | **excavation** | **metamorphic** |

1. jewel _____

2. tools _____

3. journey _____

4. resin _____

5. investigator _____

6. changed _____

7. dig _____

8. objects _____

9. record _____

10. design _____

---

**Did You Know?** The remains of Pompeii tell us about the past. When Mount Vesuvius erupted in 79 A.D., over 2000 people were unable to escape and were encased in lava. It happened so quickly that the people were killed in mid-action. The remains are being excavated to tell us about their everyday life untouched by time.

---

**Directions:** Write an **antonym** from the list of vocabulary words below on the line next to each word. An **antonym** is a word that means the opposite or nearly opposite.

|  |  |  |  |
|---|---|---|---|
| **tedious** | **relic** | **prehistoric** | **perseverance** |

1. yield _____

2. exciting _____

3. new _____     _____

**Directions:** Write a sentence for the following words on your own paper. Remember to check your spelling and punctuation.

|  |  |  |  |  |
|---|---|---|---|---|
| **archaeologist** | **historian** | **exhume** | **paleontologist** | **shards** |
| **anthropology** | **architectural** | **dating** | **sedimentary** | **igneous** |
| **ammonite** | | | | |

### Extend Your Vocabulary

1. Using plaster and shells, make your own fossil. Write down the steps it took to make one.
2. Make a list of dinosaurs; include both meat-eaters and plant-eaters.
3. Compare and contrast the architectural designs of different countries.
4. Tell about a time when you showed perseverance. Write about how you felt afterwards.

43

Name: _____     Date: _____

# Unit 11: Archaeology: *Vocabulary Quiz*

**Directions:** Match each vocabulary word with the correct meaning. Write the word on the line next to the meaning.

| | | | | |
|---|---|---|---|---|
| excavation | archaeologist | prehistoric | artifacts | lithics |
| anthropology | researcher | perseverance | archive | mosaic |
| expedition | architectural | sedimentary | shard | exhume |
| metamorphic | paleontologist | ammonite | amber | tedious |
| gemstone | igneous | historian | relic | dating |

1. _____ rock formed by the depositing of sediment

2. _____ an expert in archaeology

3. _____ journey for some special purpose

4. _____ anything made by human skill or work, especially tools or weapons

5. _____ a hard, yellow or yellowish-brown gum; resin

6. _____ the science dealing with the origin, development, races, and customs of human beings

7. _____ of the art of planning and designing buildings

8. _____ decorative design of small pieces of stone, glass, wood, etc., of different colors inlaid to form a design or picture

9. _____ rock changed in structure by heat, moisture, and pressure

10. _____ to dig out of the earth

11. _____ an expert in the science of the forms of life existing in prehistoric time, such as fossil animals and plants

12. _____ to mark with characteristics typical of a particular period; to show the age of

13. _____ rock formed by the cooling of melted rock material either within or on the surface of the earth

14. _____ of or belonging to time before histories were written

15. _____ a precious or semi-precious stone, especially when cut and polished for ornamentation; jewel

16. _____ place where public records or historical documents are kept

17. _____ coiled, flat, chambered fossil shell of an extinct mollusk

18. _____ person who does research; investigator

19. _____ thing left from the past

20. _____ sticking to a purpose or an aim

21. _____ long and tiring

22. _____ digging out; making hollow; hollowing out

23. _____ person who writes about history; expert in history

24. _____ broken pottery

25. _____ stone tools

# Unit 12: Clothing

Clothing can include any covering for a person's body. The type of clothing you wear depends on many factors. Some of these factors include the weather, time of year, occasion, and time of day. Some clothing is used for undergarments and others for outer garments. Clothing trends change and are often repeated. The clothes you wear may be very different compared to the clothes your grandparents wear. This is because you are a different age and of another generation.

clog (klog)

oxford (oks´ fərd)

babushka (bə bōosh´ kə)

waders (wā´ dərs)

bolero (bə lâr´ ō)

panama (pan´ ə mä´)

bowler (bō´ lər)

tartan (tär´ tn)

attire (ə tīr´)

frock (frok)

crinoline (krin´ ə lin)

wimple (wim´ pəl)

coronet (kôr´ ə net´)

derby (dûr´ bē)

sombrero (som brâr´ ō)

espadrille (es´ pə dril´)

periwig (per´ i wig´)

jodhpurs (jod´ pərz)

turban (tûr´ bən)

sari (sä´ rē)

kimono (kə mō´ nə)

tunic (tōo´ nik)

breeches (brēch´ iz)

kerchief (kûr´ chif)

mantilla (man tē´ yə)

# Unit 12: Clothing: *Get the Facts!*

**clog** (klog) shoe with a thick, wooden sole. *The little girl wore a pair of clogs.*

**derby** (dûr´ bē) a stiff hat with a rounded crown and narrow brim. *The Englishman liked to wear a derby.*

**oxford** (oks´ fərd) a type of low shoe, laced over the instep. *The oxfords looked good with the man's business suit.*

**sombrero** (som brâr´ ō) a broad-brimmed hat worn in the southwestern United States, Mexico, and Spain. *The man wore a sombrero to shade his head from the hot sun.*

**babushka** (bə boosh´ kə) scarf worn on the head and tied under the chin. *The Russian grandmother wore a babushka when she went outside.*

**espadrille** (es´ pə dril´) a flat sandal, usually having a fabric upper and a flexible sole. *She wore a pair of espadrilles on her vacation.*

**waders** (wā´ dərs) high, waterproof boots. *The fisherman wore waders in the stream.*

**periwig** (per´ i wig´) a wig worn in the seventeenth and eighteenth centuries. *The men wore periwigs at the trial.*

**bolero** (bə lâr´ ō) a short, loose jacket, with or without sleeves, that barely reaches to the waist. *The bullfighter wore a bolero.*

**jodhpurs** (jod´ pərz) breeches for horseback riding, loose above the knee and close-fitting below the knee. *The rider wore jodhpurs in the riding competition.*

**panama** (pan´ ə mä´) a fine hat woven from the young leaves of a palm-like plant of Central and South America. *The man from Brazil wore a panama.*

**turban** (tûr´ bən) scarf wound around the head or around a cap, worn by men in parts of India and in some other countries. *The men in India wear turbans on their heads.*

**bowler** (bō´ lər) derby. *A bowler has a dome-shaped crown.*

**sari** (sä´ rē) a long piece of cotton or silk worn wound around the body with one end thrown over the head or shoulder. *A sari is the outer garment of Hindu women.*

**tartan** (tär´ tn) a plaid cloth. *Each Scottish Highland clan has its own pattern of tartan.*

**kimono** (kə mō´ nə) a loose outer garment held in place by a sash, worn by Japanese men and women. *The Japanese lady wore a brightly colored kimono.*

**attire** (ə tīr´) clothing or dress. *The king wore rich attire to his coronation.*

**tunic** (too´ nik) garment like a skirt or gown, worn by the ancient Greeks and Romans. *The Roman emperor wore a white tunic.*

**frock** (frok) a woman's or girl's dress; robe worn by a member of the clergy; a workman's outer shirt. *The artist wore a frock.*

**breeches** (brēch´ iz) short trousers fastened below the knees. *The little boy wore breeches.*

**crinoline** (krin´ ə lin) a stiff cloth used as a lining to hold a skirt out or to make a coat collar stand up. *The lady wore a petticoat of crinoline to hold her skirt out.*

**kerchief** (kûr´ chif) piece of cloth worn over the head or around the neck. *The cowboy wore a red kerchief around his neck.*

**wimple** (wim´ pəl) cloth arranged in folds about the head, cheeks, chin, and neck. *The wimple is still worn by some nuns.*

**mantilla** (man tē´ yə) veil or scarf, often of lace, covering the hair and falling over the shoulders. *Spanish and Latin-American women sometimes wear mantillas.*

**coronet** (kôr´ ə net´) a small crown indicating a rank of nobility below that of a king or queen. *The ladies-in-waiting surrounding the queen wore coronets.*

Name: _____  Date: _____

# Unit 12: Clothing: *Skills and Practice*

**Directions:** For each word give a **synonym** from the vocabulary word list below. A **synonym** is a word that means the same or nearly the same.

| | | | |
|---|---|---|---|
| **breeches** | **periwig** | **babushka** | **waders** |
| **bolero** | **derby** | **espadrille** | **attire** |

1. water boots _____
2. clothing _____
3. bowler _____
4. scarf _____
5. knickers _____
6. sandal _____
7. wig _____
8. jacket _____

**Did You Know?** The Indian sari has no stitching, buttons, or zippers. It is a length of brightly-colored cloth that wraps around a woman's body. Even on a hot day, it is very cool and comfortable to wear.

**Directions:** Match the clothing to the correct country by placing the correct letter on the line.

_____ 1. India
_____ 2. Ancient Greece
_____ 3. Scotland
_____ 4. Mexico
_____ 5. Central/South America
_____ 6. Japan
_____ 7. Latin America

A. kimono
B. sombrero
C. panama
D. tartan
E. tunic
F. sari and turban
G. mantilla

**Directions:** Write a sentence for the following words on your own paper. Remember to check your spelling and punctuation.

| | | | | |
|---|---|---|---|---|
| **clogs** | **oxford** | **kerchief** | **frock** | **wimple** |
| **jodhpurs** | **coronet** | | | |

## Extend Your Vocabulary

1. Make a list of clothing that you wear today that was popular a long time ago.
2. Research two or more of the vocabulary words that are clothing from another country.
3. Use some of the vocabulary words from this unit to begin your own list of different types of hats. Add more to the list.
4. Design your own piece of tartan cloth. Explain the reasons for the colors and design you picked.

47

Name:_____ Date:_____

# Unit 12: Clothing: *Vocabulary Quiz*

**Directions:** Match each vocabulary word with the correct meaning. Write the word on the line next to the meaning.

| | | | | |
|---|---|---|---|---|
| clog | derby | oxford | sombrero | babushka |
| sari | waders | periwig | espadrille | jodhpurs |
| tunic | bolero | panama | breeches | coronet |
| turban | bowler | tartan | crinoline | kerchief |
| wimple | frock | attire | mantilla | kimono |

1. _____ kind of low shoe, laced over the instep

2. _____ a plaid cloth

3. _____ a wig in the seventeenth and eighteenth centuries

4. _____ clothing or dress

5. _____ a broad-brimmed hat worn in the southwestern United States, Mexico, and Spain

6. _____ a woman's or girl's dress; robe worn by a member of the clergy; a workman's outer shirt

7. _____ shoe with a thick, wooden sole

8. _____ piece of cloth worn over the head or around the neck

9. _____ a short, loose jacket, with or without sleeves, that barely reaches to the waist.

10. _____ a long piece of cotton or silk worn wound around the body with one end thrown over the head or shoulder

11. _____ a stiff hat with a rounded crown and narrow brim

12. _____ short trousers fastened below the knees

13. _____ breeches for horseback riding, loose above the knees and close-fitting below the knees

14. _____ veil or scarf, often of lace, covering the hair and falling over the shoulders

15. _____ scarf wound around the head or around a cap, worn by men in parts of India and in some other countries

16. _____ a loose outer garment held in place by a sash, worn by Japanese men and women

17. _____ scarf worn on the head and tied under the chin

18. _____ garment like a skirt or gown, worn by the ancient Greeks and Romans

19. _____ high, waterproof boots

20. _____ cloth arranged in folds about the head, cheeks, chin, and neck

21. _____ derby

22. _____ a small crown indicating a rank of nobility below that of a king or queen

23. _____ a stiff cloth used as a lining to hold a skirt out or to make a coat collar stand up

24. _____ a fine hat woven from the young leaves of a palm-like plant of Central and South America

25. _____ a flat sandal, usually having a fabric upper and a flexible sole.

48

# Unit 13: Ancient Europe

Ancient Europe includes the civilizations of Greece and Rome. They were located along the shores of the Mediterranean Sea and spread their ideas throughout many cities. The Greeks influenced the people of ancient Rome. The Romans were conquerors and built many empires throughout the continents of Europe, Asia, and Africa.

polis (pō´ lis)

agora (ag´ ə rə)

Spartan (spärt´ 'n)

forum (fôr´ əm)

plebeian (pli bē´ ən)

gladiator (glad´ ē āt´ ər)

civilization (siv´ ə lə zā´ shən)

trireme (trī´ rēm´)

empire (em´ pīr´)

revenge (ri venj´)

absolute (ab´ sə loot´)

period (pir´ ē əd)

legacy (leg´ ə sē)

helot (hel´ ət)

oligarchy (ol´ i gär´ kē)

philosophy (fə los´ ə fē)

patrician (pə trish´ ən)

tribune (trib´ yoon´)

aqueduct (ak´ wə dukt´)

oppressive (ə pres´ iv)

conquer (kon´ kər)

sculpture (skulp´ chər)

shrewd (shrood)

soothsayer (sooth´ sā´ ər)

Christianity (kris´ chē an´ ə tē)

# Unit 13: Ancient Europe: *Get the Facts!*

**polis** (pō´ lis) a city-state in ancient Greece. *Each polis had its own government.*

**helot** (hel´ ət) a person captured by Sparta and forced to live as a slave. *Helots had to farm the land.*

**agora** (ag´ ə rə) the central marketplace in ancient Athens and the site of numerous temples and government buildings. *The agora was bustling.*

**oligarchy** (ol´ i gär´ kē) a government that is run by a few people, usually by members of rich and powerful families. *The oligarchy was not a fair system.*

**Spartan** (spärt´ ʼn) person who was born in or lived in Sparta. *Spartans were trained from childhood for military service.*

**philosophy** (fə los´ ə fē) the study of the nature and purpose of life; the search for truth. *Philosophy was a part of the Greek history.*

**forum** (fôr´ əm) a marketplace in the center of ancient Rome surrounded by public buildings. *Architects designed magnificent buildings to surround the forum.*

**patrician** (pə trish´ ən) a member of a class of wealthy families who held all power in the early Roman Republic. *The Roman Senate was made up of patricians.*

**plebeian** (pli bē´ ən) a member of the common people of ancient Rome. *Plebeians were everyday people, such as farmers and merchants.*

**tribune** (trib´ yōōn´) an elected official in ancient Rome who represented the interests of the plebeians. *Tribunes held office and were elected by plebeians.*

**gladiator** (glad´ ē āt´ ər) a person, often a slave, prisoner of war, or criminal, who fought in the Roman Colosseum to entertain the public. *Sometimes gladiators fought animals.*

**aqueduct** (ak´ wə dukt´) a large stone structure built by Romans to carry water from one place to another. *The Romans built aqueducts to carry water.*

**civilization** (siv´ ə lə zā´ shən) a society that has achieved a high level of culture such as systems of government, religion, and learning. *Civilizations had different cultures.*

**oppressive** (ə pres´ iv) cruel or unjust; tyrannical. *The Spartans were oppressive to the people they conquered.*

**trireme** (trī´ rēm´) Greek sailing vessel. *The early Greeks sailed on triremes.*

**conquer** (kon´ kər) to defeat or subdue by force. *The Spartans conquered many city-states and gained their wealth.*

**empire** (em´ pīr´) a group of lands and people under one government. *The Roman Empire was expansive.*

**sculpture** (skulp´ chər) the art of making figures by carving, modeling, or casting, for example. *The tourists found great sculptures in Italy.*

**revenge** (ri venj´) harm done in return for a wrong; vengeance. *The soldiers took revenge on their enemies.*

**shrewd** (shrōōd) having a sharp mind; showing a keen wit; clever. *A shrewd Roman general defeated Hannibal.*

**absolute** (ab´ sə lōōt´) free from any imperfection or lack; whole; entire; complete. *A dictator has absolute power.*

**soothsayer** (sōōth´ sā´ ər) person who claims to foretell the future; person who predicts. *Julius Caesar consulted his soothsayer during his lifetime.*

**period** (pir´ ē əd) portion of time. *We have studied the period of Ancient Greece.*

**Christianity** (kris´ chē an´ ə tē) the religion based on the teachings of Christ as they appear in the Bible. *Christianity has the belief in one God.*

**legacy** (leg´ ə sē) something that has been handed down from an ancestor or predecessor. *The legacy of the ancient Greeks has influenced our American democracy.*

Name: _____ Date: _____

# Unit 13: Ancient Europe: *Skills and Practice*

**Directions:** For each word give a **synonym** from the vocabulary word list below. A **synonym** is a word that means the same or nearly the same.

| polis | forum | trireme | Christianity | helot |
|-------|-------|---------|--------------|-------|
| agora | tribune | absolute | revenge | gladiator |

1. religion _____       2. slave _____

3. city-state _____       4. official _____

5. fighter _____       6. vessel _____

7. whole _____       8. vengeance _____

9. marketplace _____       _____

**Did You Know?** Gladiators were usually criminals or slaves. Women were sometimes gladiators. They fought people and animals. The animals could even include elephants and giraffes.

**Directions:** Write an **antonym** from the list of vocabulary words below on the line next to each word. An **antonym** is a word that means the opposite or nearly opposite.

| shrewd | conquer | oppressive | civilization |
|--------|---------|------------|--------------|

1. gentle _____       2. surrender _____

3. ignorant _____       4. savagery _____

**Directions:** Write a sentence for the following words on your own paper. Remember to check your spelling and punctuation.

| oligarchy | Spartans | philosophy | patrician | plebeian |
|-----------|----------|------------|-----------|----------|
| aqueduct | empire | sculpture | period | legacy |

### Extend Your Vocabulary

1. Make a Venn diagram comparing Rome to Greece.
2. Make a list of Greek or Roman traditions or beliefs that have been passed down to us. Include wedding traditions.
3. Research Julius Caesar. Write a report
4. Illustrate a Roman soldier; include labels.

Name: _____ Date: _____

# Unit 13: Ancient Europe: *Vocabulary Quiz*

**Directions:** Match each vocabulary word with the correct meaning. Write the word on the line next to the meaning.

| | | | | |
|---|---|---|---|---|
| philosophy | helot | agora | oligarchy | Spartan |
| patrician | polis | forum | plebeian | tribune |
| gladiator | legacy | period | aqueduct | trireme |
| civilization | conquer | shrewd | oppressive | sculpture |
| Christianity | revenge | empire | absolute | soothsayer |

1. _____ to defeat or subdue by force

2. _____ a person captured by Sparta and forced to live as a slave

3. _____ free from any imperfection or lack; whole; entire; complete

4. _____ person who was born in or lived in Sparta

5. _____ Greek sailing vessel

6. _____ a member of the common people in ancient Rome

7. _____ portion of time

8. _____ a large stone structure built by Romans to carry water from one place to another

9. _____ the art of making figures by carving, modeling, or casting

10. _____ the central marketplace in ancient Athens and the site of numerous temples and government buildings

11. _____ person who claims to foretell the future; person who predicts

12. _____ the study of the nature and purpose of life; the search for the truth

13. _____ cruel or unjust

14. _____ a city-state in ancient Greece

15. _____ something handed down from an ancestor or predecessor

16. _____ a society that has achieved a high level of culture such as systems of government, religion, and learning

17. _____ harm done in return for a wrong; vengeance

18. _____ a marketplace in the center of ancient Rome surrounded by public buildings

19. _____ a group of lands and people under one government

20. _____ a government that is run by a few people, usually by members of rich and powerful families

21. _____ having a sharp mind; showing a keen wit; clever

22. _____ a member of a class of wealthy families who held all the power in the early Roman Republic

23. _____ the religion based on the teachings of Christ as they appear in the Bible

24. _____ a person who fought in the Roman Colosseum to entertain the public

25. _____ an elected official in ancient Rome who represented the interests of plebeians

# Unit 14: Medieval Times

Medieval times started about 500 A.D. and lasted about 1000 years. Most people were serfs and lived on large manors. The Middle Ages has also been called the Age of Faith. This is because thousands of men and women entered monasteries and convents. Trade started between Europe and the Middle East during the crusades. Towns then grew up around marketplaces, and European civilization spread.

joust (joust)

lord (lôrd)

vassal (vas´ əl)

manor (man´ ər)

convent (kon´ vənt)

pilgrimage (pil´ grim ij)

apprentice (ə pren´ tis)

Magna Carta (mag´ nə kär´ tə)

troubadour (trōō´ bə dôr´)

self-sufficient (self´ sə fish´ ənt)

artisan (ärt´ ə zən)

page (pāj)

crusade (krōō sād´)

feudalism (fyōōd´ 'l iz´ əm)

fief (fēf)

serf (sûrf)

knight (nīt)

monastery (mon´ ə ster´ ē)

guild (gild)

journeyman (jûr´ nē mən)

saint (sānt)

squire (skwīr)

minstrel (min´ strəl)

flock (flok)

influence (in´ flōō əns)

# Unit 14: Medieval Times: *Get the Facts!*

**joust** (joust) a combat with lances between two knights on horseback. *The lady gave the winner of the joust a kiss.*

**feudalism** (fyo͞od´ ′l iz´ əm) an economic and political system of Europe in the Middle Ages based on certain obligations. *Feudalism was a system to restore order and provide protection.*

**lord** (lôrd) a noble in the Middle Ages. *A serf worked for a lord in exchange for his protection and the use of his land.*

**fief** (fēf) large piece of land granted by a king to a lord in exchange for his loyalty. *In return for the fief, a lord promised to fight for the king.*

**vassal** (vas´ əl) person during the Middle Ages who promised to fight for his lord when needed, in exchange for land. *A great noble may have many vassals.*

**serf** (sûrf) person who was bound to live and work on the land of a noble. *Serfs were not free, but they were not quite slaves either.*

**manor** (man´ ər) self-sufficient farming estate where nobles and serfs lived and worked. *Almost everything needed was either made or grown on the manor.*

**knight** (nīt) son of a noble who was a trained soldier and gave military service in exchange for the right to hold land. *After serving as a page and a squire, a man was made a knight by the king.*

**convent** (kon´ vənt) a religious community in which nuns lead simple lives of work and prayer. *The young maiden entered the convent.*

**monastery** (mon´ ə ster´ ē) a religious community in which monks lead simple lives of work and prayer. *Religious men called monks worshipped in the monastery.*

**pilgrimage** (pil´ grim ij) a journey to a holy place for a religious purpose. *Many European Christians made a pilgrimage to the Holy Land.*

**guild** (gild) an organization of people who practiced the same craft, formed to set standards and promote the interests of the craft. *Weavers and shoemakers each formed guilds.*

**apprentice** (ə pren´ tis) a person who lived and worked, without pay, with a master craftsman in order to learn a trade. *During the Middle Ages, an apprentice lived in the master's house.*

**journeyman** (jûr´ nē mən) a person in the Middle Ages who had completed his apprenticeship and was paid for his work. *A journeyman had to work at least three years under a master.*

**Magna Carta** (mag´ nə kär´ tə) a document drawn up by an English noble in 1215 that spelled out certain rights and limited the king's power. *The Magna Carta was a very important document.*

**saint** (sānt) according to Roman Catholic teachings, a person believed to be especially holy. *Saint Francis was one of the most loved saints of the Middle Ages.*

**troubadour** (tro͞o´ bə dôr´) one of the lyric poets and composers of southern France, eastern Spain, and northern Italy from the 1000s to the 1200s. *The troubadours wrote mainly about love and chivalry.*

**squire** (skwīr) a young man who attended a knight until he himself became a knight. *After a page, the next step was to become a squire.*

**self-sufficient** (self´ sə fish´ ənt) asking no help; independent. *Like a manor, a monastery or a convent was self-sufficient.*

**minstrel** (min´ strəl) singer or musician in the Middle Ages who entertained the household of a noble. *The minstrels sang and recited poems.*

**artisan** (ärt´ ə zən) person skilled in some industry or trade; craftsman. *Carpenters are artisans.*

**flock** (flok) gather in a large group or crowd. *A flock of merchants gathered in the square.*

**page** (pāj) a youth who was preparing to become a knight. *A page is the first step in becoming a knight.*

**influence** (in´ flo͞o əns) power of acting on others and having an effect without using force. *The Christian church had great influence during the Middle Ages.*

**crusade** (kro͞o sād´) a series of "holy wars" in which European Christians attempted to recapture the Holy Land. *The crusades were a great failure.*

Name: _____     Date: _____

# Unit 14: Medieval Times: *Skills and Practice*

**Directions:** For each word give a **synonym** from the vocabulary word list below. A **synonym** is a word that means the same or nearly the same.

| **influence** | **guild** | **lord** | **pilgrimage** | **crusades** |
|---|---|---|---|---|
| **minstrel** | **manor** | **flock** | **self-sufficient** | **artisan** |

1. organization _____
2. noble _____
3. independent _____
4. journey _____
5. entertainer _____
6. craftsman _____
7. crowd _____
8. estate _____
9. persuade _____
10. holy wars _____

---

**Did You Know?** Each noble family had its own unique pattern on their coat of arms or shield. Each shield could have simple shapes such as stars and crosses; some had more elaborate designs such as ravens, castles, or swords. When the nobleman married, a new coat of arms was made, showing half from the man's shield and half from the woman's shield.

---

**Directions:** Write an **antonym** from the list of vocabulary words below on the line next to each word. An **antonym** is a word that means the opposite or nearly opposite.

| **knight** | **apprentice** | **saint** | **monastery** |
|---|---|---|---|

1. convent _____
2. journeyman _____
3. sinner _____
4. page _____

**Directions:** Write a sentence for the following words on your own paper. Remember to check your spelling and punctuation.

| **joust** | **feudalism** | **fief** | **vassal** | **Magna Carta** |
|---|---|---|---|---|
| **troubadour** | **serf** | | | |

## Extend Your Vocabulary

1. Research a famous person who lived during medieval times. Write a report.
2. Illustrate a shield that would represent your family.
3. What is jousting? Research it and write a mini-report.
4. Make a list of famous nuns and monks who lived during the Middle Ages.

Name: _____ Date: _____

# Unit 14: Medieval Times: *Vocabulary Quiz*

**Directions:** Match each vocabulary word with the correct meaning. Write the word on the line next to the meaning.

| joust | feudalism | lord | fief | vassal |
| monastery | pilgrimage | serf | manor | knight |
| influence | apprentice | page | flock | convent |
| journeyman | Magna Carta | saint | squire | minstrel |
| self-sufficient | troubadour | crusade | guild | artisan |

1. _____ person in the Middle Ages who had completed his apprenticeship and was paid for his work

2. _____ a noble in the Middle Ages

3. _____ an organization of people who practiced the same craft, formed to set standards and promote the interests of the craft

4. _____ a combat with lances between two knights on horseback

5. _____ according to Roman Catholic teachings, a person believed to be especially holy

6. _____ large piece of land granted by the king to a lord in exchange for his loyalty

7. _____ singer or musician in the Middle Ages who entertained the household of a noble

8. _____ son of a noble who was a trained soldier and gave military service in exchange for the right to hold land

9. _____ person who lived and worked, without pay, with a master craftsman in order to learn a trade

10. _____ person who was bound to live and work on the land of a noble

11. _____ gather in a large group or crowd

12. _____ religious community in which nuns lead simple lives of work and prayer

13. _____ a document, drawn up by an English noble in 1215, that spelled out certain rights and limited the king's power

14. _____ an economic and political system of Europe in the Middle Ages based on certain obligations

15. _____ one of the lyric poets and composers of southern France, eastern Spain, and northern Italy from the 1000s to the 1200s

16. _____ person during the Middle Ages who promised to fight for his lord when needed, in exchange for land

17. _____ person skilled in some industry or trade; craftsman

18. _____ a religious community in which monks lead simple lives of work and prayer

19. _____ young man who attended a knight until he became a knight

20. _____ self-sufficient farming estate where nobles and serfs lived and worked

21. _____ a series of "holy wars" in which European Christians attempted to recapture the Holy Land

22. _____ journey to a holy place for a religious purpose

23. _____ asking no help; independent

24. _____ power of acting on others and having an effect without using force

25. _____ a youth preparing to become a knight

# Unit 15: Energy

Energy is everywhere. It makes things happen. Energy comes in many forms, such as light, sound, movement, heat, chemical, and electrical. Energy comes from matter. Energy can never be created or destroyed; it simply changes. For example, when you run, the stored energy in your body changes into movement energy.

solar (sō´ lər)

hydroelectric (hī´ drō´ ē lek´ trik)

atom (at´ əm)

electron (ē lek´ tron´)

neutron (nōō´ tron´)

molecule (mol´ i kyōōl´)

circuit (sûr´ kit)

laser (lā´ zər)

resources (rē´ sôrs´ əz)

matter (mat´ ər)

pulley (pōōl´ ē)

renewable (ri nōō´ ə bəl)

electromagnetic (ē lek´ trō mag net´ ik)

energy (en´ ər jē)

nuclear (nōō´ klē ər)

reactor (rē ak´ tər)

proton (prō´ tän´)

deposit (di poz´ it)

radiation (rā´ dē ā´ shən)

electricity (ē´ lek tris´ i tē)

anthracite (an´ thrə sīt´)

turbine (tûr´ bin, tûr´ bīn´)

friction (frik´ shən)

lever (lev´ ər)

nonrenewable (non´ ri nōō´ ə bəl)

# Unit 15: Energy: *Get the Facts!*

**solar** (sō´ lər) of the sun. *The car runs on solar energy.*

**energy** (en´ ər jē) ability to do work; make things happen. *The sun's heat is a form of energy.*

**hydroelectric** (hī´ drō´ ē lek´ trik) developing electricity from water power. *The state gets its hydroelectric power from the huge amount of water.*

**nuclear** (noō´ klē ər) of nuclei or a nucleus, especially the nucleus of an atom. *The submarine runs on nuclear power.*

**atom** (at´ əm) the smallest particle of an element that retains the characteristics of that element. *An atom is made up of protons, neutrons, and electrons.*

**reactor** (rē ak´ tər) a vat or apparatus for the release of atomic energy by a controlled chain reaction; nuclear pile. *Reactors are needed to produce nuclear energy.*

**electron** (ē lek´ tron´) a tiny particle carrying one unit of negative electricity. *Electrons are arranged around a nucleus.*

**proton** (prō´ tän´) a tiny particle in the nucleus of the atom, carrying one unit of positive electricity. *Atoms are made up of protons, neutrons, and electrons.*

**neutron** (noō´ tron´) an atomic particle that is neutral electrically and has about the same mass as a proton. *Neutrons are in the nucleus of an atom.*

**deposit** (di poz´ it) put down; lay down. *Weathering and erosion deposit materials.*

**molecule** (mol´ i kyoōl´) smallest particle into which an element or compound can be divided without changing its chemical or physical properties. *Molecules are made up of atoms bonded together.*

**radiation** (rā´ dē ā´ shən) particles or electromagnetic waves given off by the atoms and molecules of a radio-active substance as a result of nuclear decay. *Radiation is harmful to human beings.*

**circuit** (sûr´ kit) arrangement of wiring or tubes, for example, forming electrical connections; hookup. *The circuit shorted out.*

**electricity** (ē´ lek tris´ i tē) form of energy that can produce light, heat, motion, and magnetic force. *Electricity runs most of the appliances in our homes.*

**laser** (lā´ zər) device that produces a very narrow and intense beam of light with one wavelength going in only one direction. *Lasers are used in surgery.*

**anthracite** (an´ thrə sīt´) coal that burns with very little smoke and flame; hard coal. *Anthracite can be found in layers of rock.*

**resources** (rē´ sôrs´ əz) actual and potential wealth of a country; natural resources. *Energy is a natural resource.*

**turbine** (tûr´ bin, tûr´ bīn´) engine or motor consisting of a wheel with vanes that is made to revolve by the force of water, steam, or air. *Turbines driven by falling water produce hydroelectric power.*

**matter** (mat´ ər) any physical thing; solid, liquid, or gas that takes up space. *Matter is all around us.*

**friction** (frik´ shən) force between surfaces that resists the movement of one surface past the other surface. *Friction works the brakes on a bike.*

**pulley** (poōl´ ē) simple machine made up of at least one grooved wheel and a rope, chain, or belt. *It is easy to lift a load with a pulley.*

**lever** (lev´ ər) bar that turns on a fixed support called the fulcrum and is used to transmit effort and motion. *A lever can be used to pry things open.*

**renewable** (ri noō´ ə bəl) able to be made new again; get again; fill again. *River water is renewable.*

**nonrenewable** (non´ ri noō´ ə bəl) not able to make again; cannot be replaced or fixed. *Fossil fuel is nonrenewable.*

**electromagnetic** (ē lek´ trō mag net´ ik) of or caused by an electromagnet. *Light waves are electromagnetic waves.*

Name: _____    Date: _____

# Unit 15: Energy: *Skills and Practice*

**Directions:** For each word give a **synonym** from the vocabulary word list below. A **synonym** is a word that means the same or nearly the same.

| | | | | |
|---|---|---|---|---|
| **reactor** | **energy** | **molecule** | **anthracite** | **pulley** |
| **matter** | **turbine** | **nuclear** | **deposit** | **circuit** |

1. power _____     2. coal _____

3. engine _____    4. lay down _____

5. hookup _____    6. machine _____

7. atomic _____    8. substance _____

9. particle _____  10. pile _____

**Did You Know?** If you eat a small apple, it will give you enough energy to sleep for thirty minutes.

**Directions:** Match the vocabulary word to each of the related clues. Write the word on the line.

| **radiation** | **hydroelectric** | **solar** | **resources** | **electromagnetic** |
|---|---|---|---|---|

1. sun _____       2. wealth of country _____

3. water power _____   4. radio waves _____

5. radioactive _____

**Directions:** Write a sentence for the following words on your own paper. Remember to check your spelling and punctuation.

| | | | | |
|---|---|---|---|---|
| **electricity** | **laser** | **friction** | **lever** | **nonrenewable** |
| **renewable** | **atom** | | | |

### Extend Your Vocabulary

1. Make an energy cycle. Include sun, plants, animals, and so on.
2. Using the Internet, find an experiment on energy. With a partner, perform the experiment and share with the class what you have learned.
3. Research the conservation of energy. Write a report.
4. Make a list of natural resources.

Name: _____ Date: _____

# Unit 15: Energy: *Vocabulary Quiz*

**Directions:** Match each vocabulary word with the correct meaning. Write the word on the line next to the meaning.

| | | | | |
|---|---|---|---|---|
| **deposit** | **energy** | **hydroelectric** | **nuclear** | **atom** |
| **reactor** | **electron** | **electromagnetic** | **proton** | **solar** |
| **molecule** | **radiation** | **electricity** | **neutron** | **laser** |
| **anthracite** | **resources** | **nonrenewable** | **turbine** | **matter** |
| **renewable** | **friction** | **pulley** | **lever** | **circuit** |

1. _____ actual and potential wealth of a country; natural resources

2. _____ developing electricity from water power

3. _____ form of energy that can produce light, heat, motion, and magnetic force

4. _____ tiny particle carrying one unit of negative electricity

5. _____ device that produces a very narrow and intense beam of light with one wavelength going in only one direction

6. _____ of the sun

7. _____ force between surfaces that resists the movement of one surface past the other surface

8. _____ put down; lay down

9. _____ coal that burns with very little smoke and flame; hard coal

10. _____ vat or apparatus for the release of atomic energy by a controlled chain reaction; nuclear pile

11. _____ able to be made new again; get again; fill again

12. _____ particles or electromagnetic waves given off by the atoms and molecules of a radioactive substance as a result of nuclear decay

13. _____ engine or motor consisting of a wheel with vanes that is made to revolve by the force of water, steam, or air

14. _____ ability to do work; make things happen

15. _____ bar that turns on a fixed support called the fulcrum and is used to transmit effort and motion

16. _____ an atomic particle that is neutral electrically and has about the same mass as a proton

17. _____ any physical thing; solid, liquid, or gas that takes up space

18. _____ the smallest particle of an element that retains the characteristics of that element

19. _____ not able to make again; cannot be replaced or fixed

20. _____ the smallest particle into which an element or compound can be divided without changing its chemical or physical properties

21. _____ arrangement of wiring and tubes, for example, forming electrical connections; hookup

22. _____ a tiny particle in the nucleus of the atom, carrying one unit of positive electricity

23. _____ a simple machine made up of at least one grooved wheel and a rope, chain, or belt

24. _____ of or caused by an electromagnet

25. _____ of nuclei or a nucleus, especially the nucleus of an atom

# Unit 16: Lengthy Words

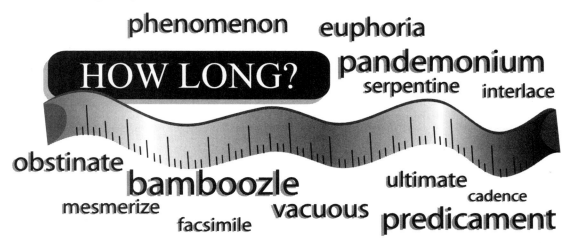

Words are all different sizes. They can be made up of one letter or many letters. Large words may often seem difficult at first; we may feel that we couldn't possibly know what they mean or how to spell them. But, in many instances, lengthy words are really made up of smaller words. This can sometimes help when it comes to figuring out their meanings.

bamboozle (bam bōō´ zəl)

enunciate (ē nun´ sē āt´)

facsimile (fak sim´ ə lē)

lethargy (leth´ ər jē)

mesmerize (mez´ mər īz´)

pandemonium (pan´ də mō´ nē əm)

quandary (kwon´ də rē)

vacuous (vak´ ū əs)

euphoria (ū fôr´ ē ə)

kleptomania (klep´ tō mā´ nē ə)

recurrence (ri kûr´ əns)

ultimate (ul´ tə mit)

phenomenon (fə nom´ ə non´)

cadence (kād´ 'ns)

interlace (in´ tər lās´)

fraudulent (frô´ jə lənt)

menagerie (mə naj´ ər ē)

metropolis (mə trop´ əl is)

predicament (pri dik´ ə mənt)

spontaneous (spon tā´ nē əs)

venomous (ven´ əm əs)

insinuate (in sin´ ū āt´)

obstinate (ob´ stə nət)

serpentine (sûr´ pən tēn´)

virtuoso (vûr´ chōō ō´ sō)

# Unit 16: Lengthy Words: *Get the Facts!*

**bamboozle** (bam bōō´ zəl) impose upon; cheat; trick. *The manager tried to bamboozle the elderly customer.*

**cadence** (kād´ 'ns) the measure or beat of music, dancing, or any movement regularly repeating itself. *The cadence of the rocker lulled the baby to sleep.*

**enunciate** (ē nun´ sē āt´) speak or pronounce words. *Television news reporters must enunciate carefully.*

**interlace** (in´ tər lās´) to unite by passing over; weave together. *The material was interlaced with gold thread.*

**facsimile** (fak sim´ ə lē) an exact copy or likeness. *We received the facsimile of the legal document today.*

**fraudulent** (frô´ jə lənt) cheating; dishonest. *The fraudulent car dealer tried to sell the lady a car.*

**lethargy** (leth´ ər jē) drowsy dullness; lack of energy. *She was in a state of lethargy after surgery.*

**menagerie** (mə naj´ ər ē) a collection of wild animals kept in cages for exhibition. *The little girl had a menagerie of glass animals.*

**mesmerize** (mez´ mər īz´) hypnotize. *The magician mesmerized the crowd.*

**metropolis** (mə trop´ əl is) a large city; important center. *We took a train to Chicago, a busy metropolis.*

**pandemonium** (pan´ də mō´ nē əm) wild uproar or confusion. *The classroom was filled with pandemonium when the teacher went to the office.*

**predicament** (pri dik´ ə mənt) an unpleasant, difficult, or bad situation. *She found herself in a predicament when her car stalled.*

**quandary** (kwon´ də rē) state of perplexity or uncertainty; dilemma. *His quandary about the new job offer was making him very upset.*

**spontaneous** (spon tā´ nē əs) caused by natural impulse or desire; not planned beforehand. *Young children often act in a spontaneous manner.*

**vacuous** (vak´ ū əs) showing no intelligence; senseless. *He made a vacuous decision when trying to cross the busy highway.*

**venomous** (ven´ əm əs) poisonous. *We stayed away from the venomous snake.*

**euphoria** (ū fôr´ ē ə) a feeling of happiness and bodily well-being. *She was in a state of euphoria when she won the race.*

**insinuate** (in sin´ u āt´) suggest in an indirect way; hint. *The principal insinuated that the class was too loud.*

**kleptomania** (klep´ tō mā´ nē ə) an abnormal, irresistible desire to steal. *He suffered from kleptomania, so he never went shopping alone.*

**obstinate** (ob´ stə nət) not giving in; stubborn. *The obstinate child refused to pick up his toys.*

**recurrence** (ri kûr´ əns) occur again; repetition. *He tried to prevent the recurrence of a flooded basement.*

**serpentine** (sûr´ pən tēn´) winding; twisting. *The serpentine road was slippery because of the rain.*

**ultimate** (ul´ tə mit) coming at the end; last; final. *The ultimate decision was made by the governor.*

**virtuoso** (vûr´ chōō ō´ sō) person skilled in the techniques of an art, especially in playing a musical instrument. *The virtuoso showed great talent when playing his violin.*

**phenomenon** (fə nom´ ə non´) fact, event, or circumstance that can be observed. *We observed a natural phenomenon.*

Name: _____    Date: _____

# Unit 16: Lengthy Words: *Skills and Practice*

**Directions:** For each word give a **synonym** from the vocabulary word list below. A **synonym** is a word that means the same or nearly the same.

| | | | |
|---|---|---|---|
| fraudulent | venomous | spontaneous | vacuous |
| facsimile | ultimate | pandemonium | quandary |
| mesmerize | recurrence | predicament | insinuate |
| bamboozle | serpentine | obstinate | |

1.  repetition _____   2.  poisonous _____

3.  copy _____   4.  hypnotize _____

5.  trick _____   6.  hint _____

7.  dishonest _____   8.  stupid _____

9.  confusion _____   10.  final _____

11.  twisting _____   12.  stubborn _____

13.  dilemma _____   _____

14.  impulsive _____

**Did You Know?** Some people read right to left and back to front. To read a book in Arabic or Hebrew, it is necessary to start on the last page reading right to left and continue to the front.

**Directions:** Write a sentence for each of the following words on your own paper. Remember to check your spelling and punctuation.

| | | | | |
|---|---|---|---|---|
| cadence | enunciate | interlace | lethargy | menagerie |
| metropolis | phenomenon | euphoria | kleptomania | virtuoso |

### Extend Your Vocabulary

1.  Make a class list of lengthy words. Look for root words that may be present.
2.  Practice with a partner enunciating a list of spelling words.
3.  Research a natural phenomenon such as "Old Faithful."
4.  Write about a time when you were in a predicament. What happened? How did you feel? How did it turn out?

63

Name: _____ Date: _____

# Unit 16: Lengthy Words: *Vocabulary Quiz*

**Directions:** Match each vocabulary word with the correct meaning. Write the word on the line next to the meaning.

| | | | | |
|---|---|---|---|---|
| **bamboozle** | **cadence** | **enunciate** | **facsimile** | **fraudulent** |
| **lethargy** | **menagerie** | **mesmerize** | **metropolis** | **pandemonium** |
| **predicament** | **quandary** | **spontaneous** | **vacuous** | **venomous** |
| **euphoria** | **insinuate** | **kleptomania** | **obstinate** | **recurrence** |
| **serpentine** | **ultimate** | **virtuoso** | **interlace** | **phenomenon** |

1. _____ suggest in an indirect way; hint

2. _____ impose upon; cheat; trick

3. _____ winding; twisting

4. _____ hypnotize

5. _____ poisonous

6. _____ to unite by passing over; weave together.

7. _____ showing no intelligence; senseless

8. _____ large city; important center

9. _____ coming at the end; last; final

10. _____ state of perplexity or uncertainty

11. _____ abnormal, irresistible desire to steal

12. _____ the measure or beat of music, dancing, or any movement regularly repeating itself

13. _____ feeling of happiness and bodily well-being

14. _____ an exact copy or likeness

15. _____ occur again; repetition

16. _____ collection of wild animals kept in cages for exhibition

17. _____ person skilled in the techniques of an art, especially in playing a musical instrument

18. _____ an unpleasant, difficult, or bad situation

19. _____ not giving in; stubborn

20. _____ cheating; dishonest

21. _____ speak or pronounce words

22. _____ wild uproar or confusion

23. _____ drowsy dullness; lack of energy

24. _____ caused by natural impulse or desire; not planned beforehand

25. _____ fact, event, or circumstance that can be observed

# Unit 17: Travel

Travel means going from one place to another. This can be done in many ways and forms. Civilization went from walking to water transportation to traveling by horse, then to wheeled vehicles, trains, and later to air travel. Traveling was often a burden, uncomfortable and time-consuming. Today you can travel very quickly to all the ends of the earth in style and luxury.

excursion (eks kûr´ zhən)

trek (trek)

caravan (kar´ ə van´)

cargo (kär´ gō)

garb (gärb)

exotic (eg zot´ ik)

outing (out´ ing)

unscheduled (un´ ske´ jŏold)

jaunt (jônt)

jet lag (jet lag)

Hoverkraft (huv´ ər kraft´)

airfare (âr´ fâr)

brochure (brō shŏor´)

bon voyage (bän´ voi äzh´)

itinerary (ī tin´ ər er´ ē)

souvenir (sōo´ və nir´)

reminiscence (rem´ ə nis´ əns)

destination (des´ tə nā´ shən)

landlubber (land´ lub´ ər)

shilling (shil´ ing)

chronicle (kron´ i kəl)

tourist (tŏor´ ist)

travelog (trav´ ə lôg´)

getaway (get´ ə wā´)

accommodations (ə kom´ ə dā´ shəns)

# Unit 17: Travel: *Get the Facts!*

**excursion** (eks kûr´ zhən) a short trip taken for interest or pleasure, often by a number of people together. *Our family went on an excursion to the mountains.*

**bon voyage** (bän´ voi äzh´) French phrase meaning pleasant journey. *Sandy's family wished her bon voyage as the ship left the dock.*

**trek** (trek) travel slowly by any means. *The pioneers trekked across the plains in covered wagons.*

**itinerary** (ī tin´ ər er´ ē) route of travel; plan of travel; record of travel; guidebook for travelers. *His itinerary was very busy and strenuous.*

**caravan** (kar´ ə van´) a group of merchants, pilgrims, and so forth traveling together for safety through difficult or dangerous country. *A caravan of merchants, with camels carrying their goods, traveled across the desert.*

**souvenir** (soo´ və nir´) something given or kept for remembrance; a keepsake. *She bought a souvenir on her trip to Washington, D.C.*

**cargo** (kär´ gō) load of goods carried by a ship or plane. *The ship carried a cargo of grain.*

**reminiscence** (rem´ ə nis´ əns) a remembering; recalling past persons or events; recollection. *His childhood reminiscences were very pleasant.*

**garb** (gärb) the way one is dressed. *She wore stylish garb on her travels.*

**destination** (des´ tə nā´ shən) a place to which a person or thing is going or is being sent. *His destination was Egypt.*

**exotic** (eg zot´ ik) foreign; strange; not native. *We saw many exotic plants in Hawaii.*

**landlubber** (land´ lub´ ər) person not used to being on ships; person who is awkward on board a ship due to lack of experience. *The landlubber was very seasick on the ship.*

**outing** (out´ ing) a short pleasure trip, walk, or airing. *Our family went on an outing to the beach.*

**shilling** (shil´ ing) a former unit of money in Great Britain equal to 12 pence or 1/20 of a pound. *A shilling was a coin used in Great Britain.*

**unscheduled** (un´ ske´ joold) not planned. *The train made an unscheduled stop.*

**chronicle** (kron´ i kəl) a record of events in the order in which they took place; history; story. *Columbus kept a chronicle of his voyages.*

**jaunt** (jônt) a short journey or excursion, especially for pleasure. *He took a jaunt to the seashore.*

**tourist** (toor´ ist) a person traveling for pleasure. *There were many tourists seeing the sights in Greece.*

**jet lag** (jet lag) the delayed effects, such as tiredness, that a person feels after a long flight in a jet plane through several time zones. *After his trip to Europe, the salesman had a case of jet lag.*

**travelog** (trav´ ə lôg´) lecture describing travel, usually accompanied by pictures or films. *He attended a travelog on Africa.*

**Hoverkraft** (huv´ ər kraft´) trademark for a vehicle that travels a few feet above the surface of land or water on a cushion of air. *There was a Hovercraft at the air show.*

**getaway** (get´ ə wā´) a period of rest and relaxation, especially a short one. *They went on a weekend getaway.*

**airfare** (âr´ fâr) the money that a person pays to ride in an airplane. *The airfare was a very reasonable price.*

**accommodations** (ə kom´ ə dā´ shəns) lodging and sometimes food as well. *Our accommodations at the motel were very enjoyable.*

**brochure** (brō shoor´) pamphlet. *She read a brochure on China.*

Name: _____  Date: _____

# Unit 17: Travel: *Skills and Practice*

**Directions:** For each word give a **synonym** from the vocabulary word list below. A **synonym** is a word that means the same or nearly the same.

| brochure | tourist | souvenir | exotic | reminiscence |
|----------|---------|----------|--------|--------------|
| caravan | chronicle | shilling | jaunt | accommodations |
| cargo | garb | | | |

1. lodging _____      2. strange _____

3. clothes _____      4. money _____

5. history _____      6. excursion _____

7. goods _____      8. recollection _____

9. keepsake _____     10. traveling group _____

11. pamphlet _____     12. vacationer _____

---

**Did You Know?** The world's longest car has 26 wheels. It actually has room for a tiny swimming pool.

---

**Directions:** Write an **antonym** from the list of vocabulary words below on the line next to each word. An **antonym** is a word that means the opposite or nearly opposite.

| landlubber | destination | unscheduled | trek |
|------------|-------------|-------------|------|

1. sailor _____      2. planned _____

3. sprint _____      4. origin _____

**Directions:** Write a sentence for the following words on your own paper. Remember to check your spelling and punctuation.

| bon voyage | itinerary | Hovercraft | jet lag | getaway |
|------------|-----------|------------|---------|---------|
| travelog | airfare | excursion | | |

### Extend Your Vocabulary

1. Make a travel brochure for an exotic getaway.
2. Make a list of at least ten national hotel chains.
3. Reminisce with a grandparent or great aunt or uncle about their childhood. Use a Venn diagram to compare their childhood to yours.
4. Describe a favorite souvenir. Where did it come from? Who bought it? What meaning does it have for you?

Name: _____ Date: _____

# Unit 17: Travel: *Vocabulary Quiz*

**Directions:** Match each vocabulary word with the correct meaning. Write the word on the line next to the meaning.

| | | | | |
|---|---|---|---|---|
| excursion | bon voyage | trek | itinerary | reminiscence |
| souvenir | caravan | cargo | destination | accommodations |
| shilling | chronicle | garb | airfare | unscheduled |
| exotic | travelog | jaunt | Hovercraft | brochure |
| jet lag | tourist | outing | getaway | landlubber |

1. _____ a short trip taken for interest or pleasure, often by a number of people together

2. _____ a short journey or excursion, especially for pleasure

3. _____ a group of merchants or pilgrims, traveling together for safety through difficult or dangerous country

4. _____ trademark for a vehicle that travels a few feet above the surface of land or water on a cushion of air

5. _____ foreign; strange; not native

6. _____ a former unit of money in Great Britain equal to 12 pence or 1/20 of a pound

7. _____ French phrase meaning pleasant journey

8. _____ record of events in the order in which they took place; history; story

9. _____ something given or kept for remembrance; a keepsake

10. _____ a short period of rest and relaxation

11. _____ a short pleasure trip, walk, or airing

12. _____ not planned

13. _____ travel slowly by any means

14. _____ the money that a person pays to ride in an airplane

15. _____ the way one is dressed

16. _____ person traveling for pleasure

17. _____ route of travel; plan of travel; record of travel; guidebook for travelers

18. _____ pamphlet

19. _____ person not used to being on ships; person who is awkward on board a ship due to lack of experience

20. _____ the delayed effects, such as tiredness, felt by a person after a long flight in a jet plane through several time zones

21. _____ load of goods carried by a ship or plane

22. _____ lecture describing travel, usually accompanied by pictures or films

23. _____ place to which a person or thing is going or is being sent

24. _____ lodging and sometimes food as well

25. _____ a remembering; recalling past persons or events; recollection

# Unit 18: Positive and Negative

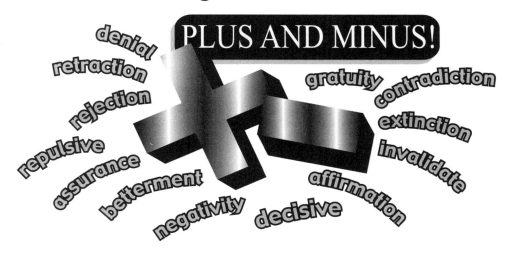

Positive is defined as permitting no question, without a doubt. Being positive can also mean showing agreement or approval. Negative is defined as stating that something is not so. It is a word or statement that says no or denies. In our language there are many ways of saying or gesturing yes and no. Another way we use positive and negative is in math.

denial (di nī´ əl)

negligence (neg´ lə jəns)

retraction (ri trak´ shən)

revoke (ri vōk´)

rejection (ri jek´ shən)

disclaimer (dis klām´ ər)

repulsive (ri pul´ siv)

assurance (ə shŏŏr´ əns)

extinguish (ek sting´ gwish)

betterment (bet´ ər mənt)

unsurpassed (un´ sər past´)

parry (par´ e)

deter (dē tûr´)

negativity (neg´ ə tiv´ ə tē)

contradiction (kon´ trə dik´ shən)

prohibition (prō´ i bish´ ən)

refusal (ri fyōō´ zəl)

affirmation (af´ ər mā´ shən)

resistant (ri zis´ tənt)

certainty (sûrt´ ’n tē)

extinction (ek stingk´ shən)

decisive (dē sī´ siv)

infallible (in fal´ ə bəl)

invalidate (in val´ ə dāt´)

gratuity (grə tōō´ i tē)

# Unit 18: Positive and Negative: *Get the Facts!*

**denial** (di nī´ əl) saying that something is not true. *He made a denial of the existence of aliens.*

**negativity** (neg´ ə tiv´ ə tē) negative quality or condition. *His negativity on the subject was apparent.*

**negligence** (neg´ lə jəns) lack of proper care or attention; neglect. *Negligence was the cause of the accident.*

**contradiction** (kon´ trə dik´ shən) denial; statement or act that contradicts another. *His actions were in contradiction to his earlier statement.*

**retraction** (ri trak´ shən) a taking back; withdrawal of a promise. *The newspaper printed a retraction about the actor.*

**prohibition** (prō´ i bish´ ən) act of forbidding by law or authority; act of preventing. *The prohibition of ice skating on the pond is sensible.*

**revoke** (ri vōk´) take back; repeal; cancel; withdraw. *The judge revoked the man's driver's license.*

**refusal** (ri fyoo´ zəl) act of refusing. *The bank president gave a refusal to lend money to him.*

**rejection** (ri jek´ shən) a rejecting; refusing to take. *The foreman ordered a rejection of all faulty parts.*

**affirmation** (af´ ər mā´ shən) positive statement; assertion. *She gave an affirmation to his decision.*

**disclaimer** (dis klām´ ər) denial; a disclaiming. *The disclaimer says the pool management is not responsible for accidents.*

**resistant** (ri zis´ tənt) resisting; opposing. *His healthy body was resistant to disease.*

**repulsive** (ri pul´ siv) causing strong dislike or aversion. *The man's crude behavior was repulsive to the woman.*

**certainty** (sûrt´ 'n tē) freedom from doubt. *The man answered the lawyer with certainty.*

**assurance** (ə shoor´ əns) statement intended to make a person more sure or certain. *I have the shipper's assurance that the package will be delivered on time.*

**extinction** (ek stingk´ shən) bringing to an end; wiping out; destruction. *Scientists and doctors are working toward the extinction of many diseases.*

**extinguish** (ek sting´ gwish) put out; bring to an end; wipe out; destroy. *Water extinguished the fire.*

**decisive** (dē sī´ siv) conclusive; critically important; showing determination or firmness. *She was decisive in her choice of food for the dinner party.*

**betterment** (bet´ ər mənt) a making better; improvement. *Fixing the old, rundown house was for the betterment of the neighborhood.*

**infallible** (in fal´ ə bəl) free from error; not able to be mistaken; sure. *We tend to think computers are infallible, but they can malfunction.*

**unsurpassed** (un´ sər past´) not capable of being improved on; superior. *His talent for golf was unsurpassed among his peers.*

**invalidate** (in val´ ə dāt´) make valueless; cause to be worthless. *The contract was invalidated because not all of the signatures were on it.*

**parry** (par´ ē) ward off; turn aside; evade. *He parried the dagger with his sword.*

**gratuity** (grə too´ i tē) present of money in return for service; tip. *Don't forget to leave a gratuity for the waitress.*

**deter** (dē tûr´) keep back; discourage or hinder. *The barking dog deterred us from entering the yard.*

Name: _____    Date: _____

# Unit 18: Positive and Negative: *Skills and Practice*

**Directions:** For each word give a **synonym** from the vocabulary word list below. A **synonym** is a word that means the same or nearly the same.

| parry | betterment | gratuity | unsurpassed | extinction |
|---|---|---|---|---|
| revoke | negligence | infallible | affirmation | disclaimer |
| deter | | | | |

1. improvement _____    2. neglect _____

3. tip _____    4. withdraw _____

5. evade _____    6. sure _____

7. hinder _____    8. superior _____

9. assertion _____    10. denial _____

11. destruction _____

---

**Did You Know?** In southern Africa children squat or sit when speaking to adults, out of respect for them.

---

**Directions:** Write an **antonym** from the list of vocabulary words below on the line next to each word. An **antonym** is a word that means the opposite or nearly opposite.

| positive | certainty | refusal | contradiction | rejection | assurance |
|---|---|---|---|---|---|

1. agreement _____    2. negative _____

3. acceptance _____    _____

4. doubt _____    _____

**Directions:** Write a sentence for the following words on your own paper. Remember to check your spelling and punctuation.

| invalidate | prohibition | retraction | resistant | repulsive |
|---|---|---|---|---|
| extinguish | decisive | denial | | |

## Extend Your Vocabulary

1. Write a short report on an animal or plant facing extinction.
2. Make a list of positive gestures.
3. Write about a time when someone was being negative and how it affected you.
4. Write a list of suggestions for the betterment of your classroom.

Name: _____  Date: _____

# Unit 18: Positive and Negative: *Vocabulary Quiz*

**Directions:** Match each vocabulary word with the correct meaning. Write the word on the line next to the meaning.

| | | | | |
|---|---|---|---|---|
| **denial** | **negativity** | **negligence** | **retraction** | **contradiction** |
| **revoke** | **rejection** | **affirmation** | **disclaimer** | **prohibition** |
| **refusal** | **resistant** | **repulsive** | **certainty** | **unsurpassed** |
| **deter** | **assurance** | **extinction** | **extinguish** | **invalidate** |
| **parry** | **gratuity** | **betterment** | **infallible** | **decisive** |

1. _____ conclusive; critically important; showing determination or firmness

2. _____ a saying that something is not true

3. _____ bringing to an end; wiping out; destruction

4. _____ a taking back; withdrawal of a promise

5. _____ statement intended to make a person more sure or certain

6. _____ positive statement; assertion

7. _____ ward off; turn aside; evade

8. _____ take back; repeal; cancel; withdraw

9. _____ put out; bring to an end; wipe out; destroy

10. _____ causing strong dislike or aversion

11. _____ keep back; discourage or hinder

12. _____ denial; statement or act that contradicts another

13. _____ a making better; improvement

14. _____ negative quality or condition

15. _____ make valueless; cause to be worthless

16. _____ a rejecting; refusing to take

17. _____ free from error; not able to be mistaken; sure

18. _____ act of forbidding by law or authority; act of preventing

19. _____ present of money in return for service; tip

20. _____ resisting; opposing

21. _____ not capable of being improved upon; superior

22. _____ freedom from doubt

23. _____ act of refusing

24. _____ lack of proper care or attention; neglect

25. _____ denial; a disclaiming

# Unit 19: Newspaper

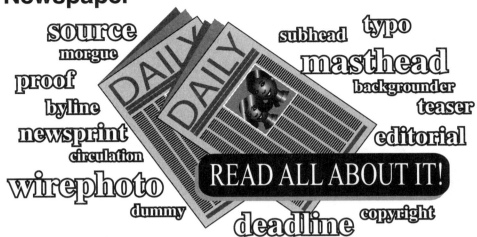

A newspaper is a daily or weekly publication printed on large pieces of paper folded together. It contains the news, advertisements, stories, pictures, and useful information. Small towns have newspapers that are published daily or weekly, while large cities have several newspapers that are published daily. The newspaper is enjoyed by a variety of people of all ages. This is because of the diversity of articles, comics, weather, sports, and more.

byline (bī′ līn′)

dummy (dum′ ē)

libel (lī′ bəl)

morgue (môrg)

teaser (tē′ zər)

Wirephoto (wīr′ fōt′ ō)

filler (fil′ ər)

backgrounder (bak′ ground′ ər)

deadline (ded′ līn′)

feature (fē′ chər)

proof (prōof)

spot news (spot nōoz)

source (sôrs)

copyright (kop′ ē rīt′)

editorial (ed′ i tôr′ ē əl)

logo (lô′ gō′)

stringer (string′ ər)

typo (tī′ pō)

masthead (mast′ hed′)

deskman (desk′ man′)

circulation (sûr′ kyōo lā′ shən)

follow-up (fol′ ō up′)

wire editor (wīr ed′ it ər)

newsprint (nōoz′ print′)

subhead (sub′ hed′)

# Unit 19: Newspaper: *Get the Facts!*

**byline** (bī´ līn´) the name of the writer printed at the head of a story. *The byline was the author's full name, John A. Smith.*

**copyright** (kop´ ē rīt´) legal protection to an author from unauthorized use of his work. *Every book has a copyright.*

**dummy** (dum´ ē) diagram of a newspaper page that shows the placement of headlines, stories, pictures, and advertisements. *The printer had trouble arranging the dummy correctly.*

**editorial** (ed´ i tôr´ ē əl) an expression of opinion of the newspaper's editors, usually that of the publisher or owner of the newspaper. *The editorial was about the coming election.*

**libel** (lī´ bəl) false communication that injures the reputation of an individual. *The newspaper was sued for libel.*

**logo** (lô´ gō´) short for "logotype," a design bearing the trademark or name of a company, business, or newspaper feature. *The golden arches is the logo for a popular fast-food restaurant.*

**morgue** (môrg) an old term for the newspaper's library where files of clippings, photos, and microfilm of past issues and other materials are contained. *The articles and pictures about the fire of 1871 were in the morgue.*

**stringer** (string´ ər) a part-time writer usually covering a particular area or subject, often paid according to the amount of his or her copy that is printed by the newspaper. *He was hired as a stringer to cover the flood.*

**teaser** (tē´ zər) an announcement placed prominently in the newspaper, often on page one, telling about an interesting story elsewhere in the paper. *The teaser was about the convention's nominee for president.*

**typo** (tī´ pō) short for "typographical error," a mistake made during the production, rather than the writing, of a story. *She found a typo in the printed article.*

**Wirephoto** (wīr´ fōt´ ō) Associated Press service that transmits pictures to subscribing newspapers. *The Wirephoto sent a picture of the robber to the newspaper.*

**masthead** (mast´ hed´) the formal statement of a paper's name, officers, point of publication, and other information, usually found on the editorial page. *Look at the masthead and tell me the newspaper's name.*

**filler** (fil´ ər) written material of minor importance used to fill extra space in the news columns. *The story on house designs was a filler in the newspaper.*

**deskman** (desk´ man´) copy editor. *The deskman is the assistant to the city or national editor.*

**backgrounder** (bak´ ground´ ər) a meeting with the press in which a source gives information not for publication, or a story that summarizes the background of a current matter in the news. *The backgrounder summarized the history of the cover-up.*

**circulation** (sûr´ kyoo lā´ shən) total number of copies of the newspaper distributed to subscribers and news vendors in a single day. *The newspaper's circulation is 40,000.*

**deadline** (ded´ līn´) the time a story must be ready to print. *The reporter had to hurry to meet the newspaper's deadline.*

**follow-up** (fol´ ō up´) a story adding more information to a story already printed. *There was a follow-up about the virus in Sunday's paper.*

**feature** (fē´ chər) a special story or article in a newspaper, often prominently displayed. *The feature article in the newspaper today was about the eclipse.*

**wire editor** (wīr ed´ it ər) person who edits news supplied by the news agencies or "wire services." *The wire editor selected stories from the wire services to use on the noon news.*

**proof** (proof) an impression of a printed page or a story. *A printer "pulls a proof" so a proofreader can check for errors.*

**newsprint** (nooz´ print´) a grade of paper made of wood pulp, used for printing newspaper. *The newsprint was delivered in large, heavy rolls.*

**spot news** (spot nooz) news obtained firsthand; fresh news. *She was at the conference to get the spot news.*

**subhead** (sub´ hed´) a one- or two-line heading used to divide sections of a story. *The story had two subheads.*

**source** (sôrs) supplier of information, such as a person, book, or survey. *He used that book as a source for his article.*

Name: _____ Date: _____

# Unit 19: Newspaper: *Skills and Practice*

**Directions:** Categorize each of the vocabulary words below and write the word on the line under the correct category.

| masthead | editorial | filler | stringer | teaser |
| feature | wire editor | logo | source | subhead |
| follow-up | deskman | | | |

**Parts of the newspaper**                    **People dealing with the newspaper**

_____                    _____

_____                    _____

_____                    _____

_____                    _____

_____

_____

_____

_____

**Did You Know?** America's first published newspaper was issued on April 24, 1704. John Campbell was the first editor.

**Directions:** Write a sentence for the following words on your own paper. Remember to check your spelling and punctuation.

| backgrounder | byline | copyright | dummy | libel |
| circulation | typo | deadline | proof | morgue |
| Wirephoto | newsprint | spot news | | |

## Extend Your Vocabulary

1. Make a class newspaper. Divide the articles and add weather, sports, comics, and so on.
2. Interview a newspaper reporter. Write about it.
3. Make a list of titles of popular newspapers.
4. Edit a partner's writing piece for errors. Use proofreading marks to make corrections.

Name: _____  Date: _____

# Unit 19: Newspaper: *Vocabulary Quiz*

**Directions:** Match each vocabulary word with the correct meaning. Write the word on the line next to the meaning.

| byline | copyright | typo | subhead | editorial |
|---|---|---|---|---|
| morgue | stringer | logo | dummy | Wirephoto |
| teaser | circulation | proof | source | deskman |
| spot news | masthead | filler | feature | backgrounder |
| deadline | wire editor | libel | follow-up | newsprint |

1. _____ the name of the writer printed at the head of a story

2. _____ written material of minor importance used to fill extra space in the news columns

3. _____ diagram of a newspaper page that shows the placement of headlines, stories, pictures, etc.

4. _____ Associated Press service that transmits pictures to subscribing newspapers

5. _____ an old term for the newspaper's library where files of clippings, photos, and microfilm of past issues and other materials are contained.

6. _____ total number of copies of the newspaper distributed to subscribers and news vendors in a single day

7. _____ an announcement placed prominently in the newspaper, often on page one, telling about an interesting story elsewhere in the paper

8. _____ formal statement of a paper's name, officers, point of publication, and other information

9. _____ legal protection to an author from unauthorized use of his work

10. _____ a special story or article in a newspaper, often prominently displayed

11. _____ short for "typographical error"

12. _____ a story that summarizes the background of a current matter in the news

13. _____ an expression of opinion of the newspaper's editors

14. _____ copy editor

15. _____ short for "logotype"

16. _____ story which adds more information to a story already printed

17. _____ news obtained firsthand; fresh news

18. _____ the time a story must be ready to print

19. _____ false communication that injures the reputation of an individual

20. _____ edits news supplied by the news agencies or "wire services"

21. _____ part-time writer, usually covering a particular area or subject, often paid according to the amount of his or her copy printed in the paper

22. _____ a grade of paper made of wood pulp, used for printing newspapers

23. _____ supplier of information, such as a person, book, or survey

24. _____ an impression of a printed page or story

25. _____ a one or two line heading used to divide sections of a story

# Unit 20: Amounts

The word *amount* can be defined as the total of two or more numbers or quantities taken together. It can also be defined as a portion or a quantity. Quantities can be very large or very small. When working with varying amounts, averages are often calculated. Averages can be reported as the mean, median, mode, and range. Amounts can be displayed through charts and graphs.

accumulate (ə kyōōm´ yə lāt´)

extensive (ek sten´ siv)

sparse (spärs)

trifle (trī´ fəl)

batch (bach)

amplitude (am´ plə tōōd´)

infinite (in´ fə nit)

monstrosity (mon stros´ ə tē)

gigantean (jī gan´ tē ən)

mean (mēn)

mode (mōd)

tinge (tinj)

scant (skant)

adequate (ad´ i kwət)

meager (mē´ gər)

surpass (sər pas´)

quantum (kwänt´ əm)

caliber (kal´ ə bər)

approximation (ə prok´ sə mā´ shən)

multitude (mul´ tə tōōd´)

voluminous (və lōōm´ ə nəs)

humongous (hyōō mong´ gəs)

median (mē´ dē ən)

scruple (skrōō´ pəl)

diminutive (də min´ yə tiv)

# Unit 20: Amounts: *Get the Facts!*

**accumulate** (ə kyo͞om´ yə lāt´) collect little by little; pile up; gather. *They accumulated enough money to buy a computer.*

**adequate** (ad´ i kwət) as much as is needed for a particlular purpose; sufficient; enough. *His allowance is adequate for his age.*

**extensive** (ek sten´ siv) of great extent; far-reaching; large. *She has an extensive collection of mystery books.*

**meager** (mē´ gər) poor or scanty. *He was still hungry after his meager meal of soup.*

**sparse** (spärs) scanty; meager. *She lives on a sparse diet of vegetables.*

**surpass** (sər pas´) do better than; be greater than; excel. *He surpasses his brother in math.*

**trifle** (trī´ fəl) small amount; little bit. *The book cost only a trifle.*

**quantum** (kwänt´ əm) basic unit of radiant energy; the smallest amount of energy capable of existing independently. *Quantum theory is based on energy.*

**batch** (bach) quantity of anything made as one lot or set; number of persons or things taken together. *She made a batch of cookies for the bake sale.*

**caliber** (kal´ ə bər) amount of ability. *He is a person of high caliber.*

**amplitude** (am´ plə to͞od´) quantity that is more than enough; abundance. *The millionaire has an amplitude of money.*

**approximation** (ə prok´ sə mā´ shən) a nearly correct amount; close estimate. *He needed an approximation of the revenue made at the fair.*

**infinite** (in´ fə nit) without limits or bounds; endless. *Do we know the infinite reaches of outer space?*

**multitude** (mul´ tə to͞od´) a great many; crowd. *There was a multitude of people at the concert.*

**monstrosity** (mon stros´ ə tē) huge; enormous. *The giant was a monstrosity.*

**voluminous** (və lo͞om´ ə nəs) of great size; large; very bulky. *A voluminous cape covered her from head to toe.*

**gigantean** (jī gan´ tē ən) like a giant; mighty; gigantic. *The basketball player is gigantean.*

**humongous** (hyo͞o mong´ gəs) extremely large; enormous. *The dinosaur in the movie looked humongous to the little boy.*

**mean** (mēn) halfway between two extremes; average. *Twelve is the mean of six and eighteen.*

**median** (mē´ dē ən) in the middle. *The median of the set {2, 6, 8, 16, 18} is 8.*

**mode** (mōd) the value or values that occur most often in a set of data. *In the set {1, 2, 3, 3, 3, 4, 4}, the mode is 3.*

**scruple** (skro͞o´ pəl) apothecary's measure of weight equal to 20 grains. *Three scruples make one dram.*

**tinge** (tinj) a very small amount; trace. *She likes a tinge of cream in her coffee.*

**diminutive** (də min´ yə tiv) very small; tiny; minute. *The dollhouse had diminutive furniture.*

**scant** (skant) barely enough; barely full; bare. *Use a scant cup of margarine in the cake.*

Name: _____     Date: _____

# Unit 20: Amounts: *Skills and Practice*

**Directions:** For each word give a **synonym** from the vocabulary word list below. A **synonym** is a word that means the same or nearly the same.

| | | | | |
|---|---|---|---|---|
| **meager** | **amplitude** | **humongous** | **multitude** | **median** |
| **trifle** | **diminutive** | **approximation** | **extensive** | **surpass** |
| **mean** | | | | |

1. monstrosity_____     2. sparse_____
3. excel _____     4. far-reaching _____
5. tinge _____     6. abundance _____
7. estimate _____     8. middle _____
9. average _____     10. minute _____
11. crowd _____

> **Did You Know?** When averaging numbers, the minimum is the smallest value and the maximum is the largest value. Cherrapunji, India, is one of the world's wettest places, receiving a maximum average of nearly 430 inches of rain per year.

**Directions:** Write an **antonym** from the list of vocabulary words below on the line next to each word. An **antonym** is a word that means the opposite or nearly opposite.

| | | | |
|---|---|---|---|
| **infinite** | **adequate** | **scant** | **accumulate** |

1. insufficient _____     2. disperse _____
3. limited _____     4. plentiful _____

**Directions:** Write a sentence for the following words on your own paper. Remember to check your spelling and punctuation.

| | | | | |
|---|---|---|---|---|
| **batch** | **voluminous** | **caliber** | **scruple** | **monstrosity** |
| **mode** | **gigantean** | **sparse** | **tinge** | |

## Extend Your Vocabulary

1. Read the book *How Much is a Million.* Write a reaction.
2. Make two lists of words, one meaning "large" and one meaning "small."
3. Find a *Guinness Book of World Records* and record some very large or very small records.
4. Read some fairy tales that have gigantean characters. List them.

Name:_____ Date:_____

# Unit 20: Amounts: *Vocabulary Quiz*

**Directions:** Match each vocabulary word with the correct meaning. Write the word on the line next to the meaning.

| | | | | |
|---|---|---|---|---|
| meager | accumulate | mean | extensive | approximation |
| sparse | amplitude | infinite | multitude | monstrosity |
| trifle | humongous | scant | caliber | voluminous |
| batch | gigantean | median | surpass | diminutive |
| mode | scruple | tinge | quantum | adequate |

1. _____ in the middle

2. _____ as much as is needed for a particlular purpose; sufficient; enough

3. _____ of great size; large; very bulky

4. _____ scanty; meager

5. _____ extremely large; enormous

6. _____ collect little by little; pile up; gather

7. _____ apothecary's measure of weight equal to 20 grains

8. _____ amount of ability

9. _____ halfway between two extremes; average

10. _____ of great extent; far-reaching; large

11. _____ a very small amount; trace

12. _____ the basic unit of radiant energy; the smallest amount of energy capable of existing independently

13. _____ like a giant; mighty; gigantic

14. _____ huge; enormous

15. _____ barely enough; barely full; bare

16. _____ quantity of anything made as one lot or set; number of persons or things taken together

17. _____ the value or values that occur most often in a set of data

18. _____ do better than; be greater than; excel

19. _____ very small; tiny; minute

20. _____ a great many; crowd

21. _____ a small amount; little bit

22. _____ without limits or bounds; endless

23. _____ poor or scanty

24. _____ quantity that is more than enough; abundance

25. _____ a nearly correct amount; estimate

# Unit 21: Peace and War

Since the beginning of time, people have lived in times of peace and war. Money, land, and power have always been at the center of war. The United Nations, a worldwide organization, was formed in 1945 to promote worldwide peace. It now has over 140 members; its headquarters is in New York City.

disturbance (di stûr´ bəns)

justice (jus´ tis)

quarrel (kwôr´ əl)

intolerance (in tol´ ər əns)

chaos (kā´ os´)

truce (tro͞os)

animosity (an´ ə mos´ ə tē)

strife (strīf)

injustice (in jus´ tis)

placid (plas´ id)

tactic (tak´ tik)

bellicose (bel´ i kōs´)

arbitration (är´ bə trā´ shən)

discord (dis´ kôrd)

antagonism (an tag´ ə niz´ əm)

cooperative (kō op´ ər ə tiv)

tranquillity (trang kwil´ ə tē)

serenity (sə ren´ ə tē)

harmony (här´ mə nē)

amicable (am´ i kə bəl)

tolerance (tol´ ər əns)

humanity (hyo͞o man´ ə tē)

amity (am´ i tē)

combative (kəm bat´ iv)

tyrannical (tə ran´ i kəl)

# Unit 21: Peace and War: *Get the Facts!*

**disturbance** (di stûr´ bəns) a disturbing or a being disturbed; disorder; confusion. *There was a disturbance at the football game.*

**discord** (dis´ kôrd) a difference of opinion; disagreement; disputing. *The argument caused discord among the group.*

**justice** (jus´ tis) just conduct; fair dealing; fairness. *He has a sense of justice and conducts the meetings fairly.*

**antagonism** (an tag´ ə niz´ əm) active opposition; hostility. *The prisoner's antagonism of the guard only made the situation worse.*

**quarrel** (kwôr´ əl) an angry dispute; a fight with words. *The two girls had a quarrel over something trivial.*

**cooperative** (kō op´ ər ə tiv) wanting or willing to work together with others. *Her students were very cooperative.*

**intolerance** (in tol´ ər əns) unwillingness to let others do and think as they choose. *The Pilgrims came to America because of religious intolerance in their homeland.*

**tranquillity** (trang kwil´ ə tē) calmness; peacefulness; quiet. *She loved the tranquillity of the lake.*

**chaos** (kā´ os´) very great confusion; complete disorder. *The twister left the town in chaos.*

**serenity** (sə ren´ ə tē) peace and quiet; calmness. *There was a sense of serenity as she strolled through the flower conservatory.*

**truce** (trōōs) a stop in fighting; temporary peace. *A truce was announced by the two warring countries.*

**harmony** (här´ mə nē) agreement of feelings, ideas, or actions; getting on well together. *The two sisters lived in perfect harmony.*

**animosity** (an´ ə mos´ ə tē) violent hatred; active dislike. *The animosity of the two men was very evident.*

**amicable** (am´ i kə bəl) having or showing a friendly attitude; peaceable. *The two companies settled their disagreement in an amicable way.*

**strife** (strīf) a quarreling; fighting. *There was bitter strife between the two rivals.*

**tolerance** (tol´ ər əns) a willingness to be tolerant; a putting up with people whose opinions or ways differ from one's own. *He had a tolerance for different faiths.*

**injustice** (in jus´ tis) being unjust; lack of justice. *It is an injustice to accuse someone of a crime without proof.*

**humanity** (hyōō man´ ə tē) human beings; people; mankind. *Humanity has made great advances in technology.*

**placid** (plas´ id) pleasantly calm or peaceful; quiet. *The placid lake was very inviting to the tourist.*

**amity** (am´ i tē) peace and friendship. *If there is amity between friends, there are no arguments.*

**tactic** (tak´ tik) maneuver. *The tactic of pretending to retreat fooled the enemy.*

**combative** (kəm bat´ iv) ready to fight; fond of fighting. *The irritated man was in a very combative mood.*

**bellicose** (bel´ i kōs´) fond of fighting; warlike. *In ancient Rome, the gladiators were bellicose fighters.*

**tyrannical** (tə ran´ i kəl) of or like a tyrant; cruel; unjust. *The people despised their tyrannical queen.*

**arbitration** (är´ bə trā´ shən) settlement of a dispute by the decision of a judge, umpire, or committee. *The two quarreling parties went into arbitration to settle their differences.*

Name: _____  Date: _____

# Unit 21: Peace and War: *Skills and Practice*

**Directions:** For each word give a **synonym** from the vocabulary word list below. A **synonym** is a word that means the same or nearly the same.

| | | | | |
|---|---|---|---|---|
| **bellicose** | **humanity** | **chaos** | **disturbance** | **justice** |
| **injustice** | **tyrannical** | **tactic** | **serenity** | **harmony** |
| **arbitration** | **tranquillity** | | | |

1. cruel _____
2. mankind _____
3. maneuver _____
4. combative _____
5. agreement _____
6. partiality _____
7. fairness _____
8. settlement _____
9. disorder _____   _____
10. calmness _____   _____

---

**Did You Know?** The Maori people of New Zealand stick out their tongues to say "hello." They welcome guests by staring at them fiercely and sticking out their tongues.

---

**Directions:** Write an **antonym** from the list of vocabulary words below on the line next to each word. An **antonym** is a word that means the opposite or nearly opposite.

| | | | | |
|---|---|---|---|---|
| **animosity** | **intolerance** | **placid** | **discord** | **amicable** |

1. agreement _____
2. love _____
3. noisy _____
4. warlike _____
5. cooperative _____

**Directions:** Write a sentence for the following words on your own paper. Remember to check your spelling and punctuation.

| | | | | |
|---|---|---|---|---|
| **amity** | **antagonism** | **quarrel** | **tolerance** | **strife** |
| **truce** | **cooperative** | **combative** | | |

## Extend Your Vocabulary

1. Make a list of symbols of peace. Illustrate some of them, for example: peace sign, handshake.
2. Research the Peace Corps and what it stands for. Write a report.
3. Discuss the meaning of the figurative phrase, "to hold one's peace."
4. List the reasons for World War I and World War II.

Name: _____   Date: _____

# Unit 21: Peace and War: *Vocabulary Quiz*

**Directions:** Match each vocabulary word with the correct meaning. Write the word on the line next to the meaning.

| | | | | |
|---|---|---|---|---|
| cooperative | intolerance | chaos | serenity | tranquillity |
| animosity | amicable | truce | discord | disturbance |
| antagonism | humanity | strife | justice | tolerance |
| injustice | combative | amity | tactic | bellicose |
| tyrannical | arbitration | placid | quarrel | harmony |

1. _____ human beings; people; mankind

2. _____ a disturbing or a being disturbed; disorder; confusion

3. _____ a quarreling; fighting

4. _____ very great confusion; complete disorder

5. _____ being unjust; lack of justice

6. _____ active opposition; hostility

7. _____ a willingness to be tolerant; a putting up with people whose opinions or ways differ from one's own

8. _____ calmness; peacefulness; quiet

9. _____ pleasantly calm or peaceful; quiet

10. _____ peace and quiet; calmness

11. _____ of or like a tyrant; cruel; unjust

12. _____ a stop in fighting; temporary peace

13. _____ peace and friendship

14. _____ wanting or willing to work together with others

15. _____ fond of fighting; warlike

16. _____ having or showing a friendly attitude; peaceable

17. _____ settlement of a dispute by the decision of a judge, umpire, or committee

18. _____ a difference of opinion; disagreement; disputing

19. _____ maneuver

20. _____ an angry dispute; a fight with words

21. _____ ready to fight; fond of fighting

22. _____ unwillingness to let others do and think as they choose

23. _____ just conduct; fair dealing; fairness

24. _____ violent hatred; active dislike

25. _____ agreement of feeling, ideas, or actions; getting on well together

# Unit 22: Health

The body is able to look after itself. It has defenses against disease and the power to repair itself. Our body does, however, need maintenance. Keeping healthy includes eating a balanced diet and exercising. Avoiding harmful habits such as smoking also helps. To keep your whole body healthy and clean you need to brush your teeth, take baths and showers, and wash your hair.

contagious (kən tā´ jəs)

convalescence (kon´ və les´ əns)

laceration (las´ ər ā´ shən)

chemotherapy (kē´ mō ther´ ə pē)

heredity (hə red´ i tē)

life span (līf span)

neuron (noo´ ron´)

quarantine (kwôr´ ən tēn)

sterilization (ster´ ə li zā´ shən)

vaccination (vak´ sə nā´ shən)

hygiene (hī´ jēn´)

contaminated (kən tam´ ə nāt´ ed)

diagnosis (dī´ əg nō´ sis)

paralysis (pə ral´ ə sis)

coronary (kôr´ ə ner´ ē)

tetanus (tet´ 'n əs)

gene (jēn)

immunity (i myoon´ i tē)

metabolism (mə tab´ ə liz´ əm)

pituitary (pi too´ ə ter´ ē)

respiration (res´ pə rā´ shən)

synapse (sin´ aps´)

vigor (vig´ ər)

epidemic (ep´ ə dem´ ik)

antibiotic (an´ tī bī ot´ ik)

# Unit 22: Health: *Get the Facts!*

**contagious** (kən tā´ jəs) spreading by contact; catching. *Chicken pox is a contagious disease.*

**paralysis** (pə ral´ ə sis) a lessening or loss of the power of motion or sensation in any part of the body. *The car accident caused paralysis in the driver.*

**convalescence** (kon´ və les´ əns) the gradual recovery of health and strength after an illness. *The doctor prescribed a two-week convalescence at home for his patient.*

**coronary** (kôr´ ə ner´ ē) of or having to do with either of the two arteries that supply blood to the muscular tissue of the heart. *The old man had a blocked coronary artery.*

**laceration** (las´ ər ā´ shən) a rough tear; mangled place. *A torn, jagged wound is a laceration.*

**tetanus** (tet´ ’n əs) disease caused by certain bacteria usually entering the body through wounds, characterized by violent spasms and stiffness of many muscles. *Tetanus of the jaw muscles is called lockjaw.*

**chemotherapy** (kē´ mō ther´ ə pē) the use of chemical agents in the treatment or control of disease. *The cancer patient needed chemotherapy.*

**gene** (jēn) a minute part of a chromosome that influences the inheritance and development of some characteristic. *Your genes are inherited from your parents.*

**heredity** (hə red´ i tē) the passing on of physical or mental characteristics from parent to offspring by means of genes. *Freckles are a part of heredity.*

**immunity** (i myōōn´ i tē) resistance to disease or poison. *The vaccination gave the child an immunity to the disease.*

**life span** (līf span) the period between birth and death during which a living thing is functional. *She had a long and prosperous life span.*

**metabolism** (mə tab´ ə liz´ əm) process by which all living things turn food into energy and living tissue. *Metabolism causes food to break down to produce energy.*

**neuron** (nōō´ ron´) one of the cells of which the brain, spinal cord, and nerves are composed; nerve cell. *Neurons conduct impulses.*

**pituitary** (pi tōō´ ə ter´ ē) a small, oval endocrine gland situated at the base of the brain. *The pituitary gland secretes hormones that promote growth.*

**quarantine** (kwôr´ ən tēn) kept away from others for a time to prevent the spread of an infectious disease. *If you have smallpox, you will be quarantined.*

**respiration** (res´ pə rā´ shən) act of inhaling and exhaling; breathing. *A severe cold can make respiration difficult.*

**sterilization** (ster´ ə li zā´ shən) free from living germs. *The autoclave is used for the sterilization of surgical instruments.*

**synapse** (sin´ aps´) place where a nerve impulse passes from one nerve cell to another. *The two nerve endings meet at the synapse.*

**vaccination** (vak´ sə nā´ shən) inoculate with a vaccine. *Vaccination has made smallpox a very rare disease.*

**vigor** (vig´ ər) active strength or force. *The wrestler was full of vigor.*

**hygiene** (hī´ jēn´) rules of health; the science of keeping well. *Good hygiene is important for a healthy life.*

**epidemic** (ep´ ə dem´ ik) the rapid spread of disease so that many people have it at the same time. *There was an epidemic of measles.*

**contaminated** (kən tam´ ə nāt´ ed) made impure by contact; defiled; polluted. *The water was contaminated by waste.*

**antibiotic** (an´ tī bī ot´ ik) substance produced by a living organism, especially a bacterium or fungus, that destroys or weakens germs. *Penicillin is an antibiotic.*

**diagnosis** (dī´ əg nō´ sis) act or process of determining the type of illness or disease of a person or animal by examination and careful study of the symptoms. *The doctor's diagnosis was that the girl had a virus.*

Name: _____  Date: _____

# Unit 22: Health: *Skills and Practice*

**Directions:** For each word give a **synonym** from the vocabulary word list below. A **synonym** is a word that means the same or nearly the same.

| coronary | contagious | respiration | convalescence | epidemic |
|---|---|---|---|---|
| laceration | sterilization | immunity | contaminated | vigor |
| diagnosis | vaccination | | | |

1.  catching _____
2.  recovery _____
3.  tear _____
4.  resistance _____
5.  inoculation _____
6.  breathing _____
7.  heart _____
8.  strength _____
9.  germ-free _____
10. polluted _____
11. analysis _____
12. infestation _____

**Did You Know?** Earl Dickerson invented the Band-Aid. He put small squares of cloth onto pieces of tape, covering them completely to stop the glue from drying out.

**Directions:** Read the following list of words and circle those that are parts of the human body.

**synapse    gene    hygiene    neuron    heredity    pituitary    life span**

**Directions:** Write a sentence for the following words on your own paper. Remember to check your spelling and punctuation.

| paralysis | tetanus | chemotherapy | heredity | gene |
|---|---|---|---|---|
| lifespan | synapse | contaminated | hygiene | neuron |
| pituitary | antibiotic | metabolism | quarantine | |

### Extend Your Vocabulary

1.  Make a list of contagious ailments.
2.  Invite a doctor or nurse to your school. Have a question and answer session.
3.  Research vaccinations and why children need them.
4.  As a class, visit a younger classroom and explain good hygiene.

Name: _____ Date: _____

# Unit 22: Health: *Vocabulary Quiz*

**Directions:** Match each vocabulary word with the correct meaning. Write the word on the line next to the meaning.

| | | | | |
|---|---|---|---|---|
| contagious | paralysis | convalescence | coronary | gene |
| tetanus | laceration | chemotherapy | heredity | vigor |
| immunity | metabolism | contaminated | life span | neuron |
| synapse | pituitary | quarantine | hygiene | epidemic |
| antibiotic | respiration | sterilization | vaccination | diagnosis |

1. _____ one of the cells of which the brain, spinal cord, and nerves are composed; nerve cell

2. _____ the gradual recovery of health and strength after an illness

3. _____ free from living germs

4. _____ the use of chemical agents in the treatment or control of disease

5. _____ active strength or force

6. _____ resistance to disease or poison

7. _____ act of inhaling and exhaling; breathing

8. _____ spreading by contact; catching

9. _____ keep away from others for a time to prevent the spread of an infectious disease

10. _____ of or having to do with either of the two arteries that supply blood to the muscular tissue of the heart

11. _____ a small, oval endocrine gland situated at the base of the brain

12. _____ a minute part of a chromosome that influences the inheritance and development of some characteristic

13. _____ made impure by contact; defiled; polluted

14. _____ process by which all living things turn food into energy and living tissue

15. _____ place where a nerve impulse passes from one nerve cell to another

16. _____ a lessening or loss of the power of motion or sensation in any part of the body

17. _____ inoculate with a vaccine

18. _____ a rough tear; mangled place

19. _____ the rapid spread of disease so that many people have it at the same time

20. _____ the passing on of physical or mental characteristics from parent to offspring by means of genes

21. _____ substance produced by a living organism, especially a bacterium or fungus, that destroys or weakens germs

22. _____ the period between birth and death during which a living thing is functional

23. _____ rules of health; science of keeping well

24. _____ disease caused by certain bacteria, usually entering the body through wounds, characterized by violent spasms and stiffness of many muscles

25. _____ act or process of determining the type of illness or disease of a person or animal by examination and careful study of the symptoms

# Unit 23: Movement

Movement is the changing of place or position. Our muscles allow us to move. You can move at any pace; sometimes you move at a brisk pace, while at other times you are nearly motionless. You may linger, totter, scurry, or straggle. If you walk for an hour without taking a break, you will have walked about two and one-half miles. You need energy to move.

brisk (brisk)

linger (ling´ gər)

nimble (nim´ bəl)

scurry (skûr´ ē)

recede (ri sēd´)

tread (tred)

fluctuate (fluk´ choo āt´)

hover (huv´ ər)

deviate (dē´ vē āt´)

fidgety (fij´ it ē)

roving (rōv´ ing)

canter (kant´ ər)

scuttle (skut´ ′l)

fleet (flēt)

mingle (ming´ gəl)

perpetual (pər pech´ oo əl)

totter (tot´ ər)

transverse (trans vûrs´)

gait (gāt)

mobility (mō bil´ ə tē)

kinesthetic (kin´ is thet´ ik)

propel (prə pel´)

flurry (flûr´ ē)

straggle (strag´ əl)

acceleration (ak sel´ ər ā´ shən)

# Unit 23: Movement: *Get the Facts!*

**brisk** (brisk) quick and active; lively. *She takes a brisk walk every morning.*

**fleet** (flēt) swiftly moving; rapid. *The fleet horse galloped away.*

**linger** (ling´ gər) stay on; leave slowly. *He lingered at his friend's house after everyone else had left.*

**mingle** (ming´ gəl) combine in a mixture; mix; blend. *The artist mingled the two colors to create a new shade of blue.*

**nimble** (nim´ bəl) active and sure-footed; quick; agile. *The mountain lion is a nimble climber.*

**perpetual** (pər pech´ oo əl) never ceasing; continuous. *She had a perpetual stream of visitors at the hospital.*

**scurry** (skûr´ ē) run quickly; scamper; hurry. *The mouse scurried across the floor.*

**totter** (tot´ ər) walk with shaky, unsteady steps. *The baby tottered across the room.*

**recede** (ri sēd´) go backward; move backward. *We dug for shells when the tide receded.*

**transverse** (trans vûrs´) lying across; placed crosswise; crossing from side to side. *The building needed transverse beams for support.*

**tread** (tred) set the foot down; walk; step. *Be careful not to tread on the flowers.*

**gait** (gāt) the kind of steps used in going along; manner of walking or running. *Grandma has a slow gait.*

**fluctuate** (fluk´ choo āt´) rise and fall; change continually; waver. *The temperature fluctuates each day.*

**mobility** (mō bil´ ə tē) ability or readiness to move or be moved. *The elderly man's mobility was amazing.*

**hover** (huv´ ər) stay in or near one place in the air. *The hummingbird hovered over the flower.*

**kinesthetic** (kin´ is thet´ ik) having to do with sensations of motion from the muscles and joints. *The student was a kinesthetic learner.*

**deviate** (dē´ vē āt´) turn aside from a way, course, truth, and so on. *The parade deviated from its planned course.*

**propel** (prə pel´) drive forward; force ahead. *He propels the boat by oars.*

**fidgety** (fij´ it ē) restless; uneasy. *The fidgety child kept moving around during the concert.*

**flurry** (flûr´ ē) a sudden gust. *A flurry of wind toppled the small sailboat.*

**roving** (rōv´ ing) wandering about; roaming; rambling. *She was roving through the woods looking for berries.*

**straggle** (strag´ əl) wander in a scattered fashion. *The chickens straggled along the road.*

**canter** (kant´ ər) gallop gently. *The boy cantered his pony down the road.*

**acceleration** (ak sel´ ər ā´ shən) a speeding up or hastening. *The acceleration of his heartbeat was caused by a shock.*

**scuttle** (skut´ 'l) scamper; scurry. *The squirrels scuttled off to the woods.*

Name: _____  Date: _____

# Unit 23: Movement: *Skills and Practice*

**Directions:** For each word give a **synonym** from the vocabulary word list below. A **synonym** is a word that means the same or nearly the same.

| canter | roving | tread | mingle | scurry |
|--------|--------|-------|--------|--------|
| fidgety | flurry | brisk | fleet | |

1. scuttle _____
2. gust _____
3. roaming _____
4. restless _____
5. gallop _____
6. rapid _____
7. walk _____
8. lively _____
9. mix _____

**Did You Know?** If you stayed in bed all day, you would still travel about 1.5 million miles. That is how far the earth moves through space in 24 hours as it goes around the sun.

**Directions:** Write an **antonym** from the list of vocabulary words below on the line next to each word. An **antonym** is a word that means the opposite or nearly opposite.

| mobility | acceleration | nimble | recede | linger |
|----------|--------------|--------|--------|--------|
| fluctuate | perpetual | | | |

1. deceleration _____
2. hasten _____
3. propel _____
4. remain _____
5. immobility _____
6. temporary _____
7. awkward _____

**Directions:** Write a sentence for the following words on your own paper. Remember to check your spelling and punctuation.

| totter | transverse | gait | hover | deviate |
|--------|------------|------|-------|---------|
| straggle | kinesthetic | propel | scuttle | |

## Extend Your Vocabulary

1. Categorize this unit's words under certain headings, such as slow and fast movements.
2. Match as many of the movements as you can with a particular animal, such as hover - hummingbird; scurry - mouse, and so on.
3. Research the different muscles and how they allow our body to move. Write a report.
4. Make a list of oxymorons such as these: restless sleep, gentle turbulence, slow jet.

Name: _____   Date: _____

# Unit 23: Movement: *Vocabulary Quiz*

**Directions:** Match each vocabulary word with the correct meaning. Write the word on the line next to the meaning.

| brisk | perpetual | fluctuate | fleet | linger |
| nimble | transverse | mobility | tread | flurry |
| scurry | kinesthetic | deviate | hover | canter |
| roving | acceleration | propel | recede | scuttle |
| totter | straggle | fidgety | mingle | gait |

1. _____ turn aside from a way, course, truth, and so on.

2. _____ swiftly moving; rapid

3. _____ having to do with sensations of motion from the muscles and joints

4. _____ never ceasing; continuous

5. _____ a speeding up or hastening

6. _____ lying across; placed crosswise; crossing from side to side

7. _____ restless; uneasy

8. _____ stay on; go slowly

9. _____ drive forward; force ahead

10. _____ quick and active; lively

11. _____ wander in a scattered fashion

12. _____ rise and fall; change continually; waver

13. _____ scamper; scurry

14. _____ stay in or near one place in the air

15. _____ wandering about; roaming; rambling

16. _____ walk with shaky, unsteady steps

17. _____ a sudden gust

18. _____ active and sure-footed; quick; agile

19. _____ gallop gently

20. _____ to combine in a mixture; mix; blend

21. _____ ability or readiness to move or be moved

22. _____ run quickly; scamper; hurry

23. _____ the kind of steps used in going along; manner of walking or running

24. _____ go backward; move backward

25. _____ set the foot down; walk; step

# Unit 24: Law

For people to survive, a system of rules had to be formed to protect society. Laws may be made by a country or a state, for example. Without laws there is disorder and bedlam. Laws are often broken. We have a judicial system in place that includes judges, lawyers, defendants and plaintiffs. Laws are not concrete; they may be interpreted in many ways. As a result, every day lawsuits are filed and courtrooms are busy throughout our land.

defendant (dē fen´ dənt)

penitentiary (pen´ i ten´ shə rē)

testimony (tes´ tə mō´ nē)

witness (wit´ nis)

opponent (ə pō´ nənt)

allegation (al´ ə gā´ shən)

subpoena (sə pē´ nə)

law-abiding (lȯ´ ə bīd´ ing)

lawsuit (lȯ´ so͞ot)

bungling (bung´ gling)

legitimate (lə jit´ ə mət)

bylaw (bī´ lȯ´)

legality (li gal´ i tē)

evidence (ev´ ə dəns)

larceny (lär´ sə nē)

verdict (vûr´ dikt)

objection (əb jek´ shən)

conviction (kən vik´ shən)

attest (ə test´)

sequester (si kwes´ tər)

accomplice (ə kom´ plis)

disposition (dis´ pə zish´ ən)

culprit (kul´ prit)

summation (sə mā´ shən)

habeas corpus (hā´ bē əs kôr´ pəs)

# Unit 24: Law: *Get the Facts!*

**defendant** (dē fen´ dənt) person accused in a court of law. *The defendant is charged with robbery.*

**evidence** (ev´ ə dəns) anything that shows what is true and what is not; facts; proof. *The evidence proved that he was guilty.*

**penitentiary** (pen´ i ten´ shə rē) a prison for criminals. *The murderer was sent to the state penitentiary.*

**larceny** (lär´ sə nē) the unlawful taking and using of the personal property of another person; theft. *The man committed larceny when he stole the computer.*

**testimony** (tes´ tə mō´ nē) statement used for evidence; proof. *The witness's testimony helped convict the defendant.*

**verdict** (vûr´ dikt) the decision of a jury. *The jury's verdict was "guilty."*

**witness** (wit´ nis) person who saw something happen; spectator; eyewitness. *There were several witnesses to the crime.*

**objection** (əb jek´ shən) something said in objecting; reason or argument against something. *The lawyer had an objection to the question.*

**opponent** (ə pō´ nənt) person who is on the other side in a fight, game, or discussion; person fighting, struggling, or speaking against another. *He was an opponent of the killing of animals for fur coats.*

**conviction** (kən vik´ shən) act of proving or declaring guilty. *The trial resulted in the conviction of the accused woman.*

**allegation** (al´ ə gā´ shən) an accusation made without proof. *The allegations against her were serious.*

**attest** (ə test´) give proof of; certify; bear witness; testify. *The expert attested to the fact that the handwriting was genuine.*

**subpoena** (sə pē´ nə) an official written order commanding a person to appear in a court of law. *She was served a subpoena from the court official.*

**sequester** (si kwes´ tər) remove or withdraw from public use or from public view. *The jury was sequestered until the trial was over.*

**law-abiding** (lô´ ə bīd´ ing) obeying the law; peaceful and orderly. *She was a law-abiding citizen.*

**accomplice** (ə kom´ plis) person who knowingly aids another in committing a crime or other wrong act. *She was an accomplice to her husband's robbery.*

**lawsuit** (lô´ sōot) case in a court of law started by one person to claim something from another. *She filed a lawsuit against the company for her injuries.*

**disposition** (dis´ pə zish´ ən) a disposing; settlement. *What was the disposition of the case?*

**bungling** (bung´ gling) do or make in a clumsy, unskilled way. *The investigator was always bungling his cases.*

**culprit** (kul´ prit) person guilty of a fault or crime; offender. *Was he the culprit of the crime?*

**legitimate** (lə jit´ ə mət) allowed or admitted by law; rightful; lawful. *She had a legitimate right to the money left in her father's will.*

**summation** (sə mā´ shən) the final presentation of facts and arguments by the counsel for each side. *In his summation, the lawyer reviewed the evidence.*

**bylaw** (bī´ lô´) law made by a city, company, club, and so forth for the control of its own affairs. *She read the club's bylaws at the meeting.*

**habeas corpus** (hā´ bē əs kôr´ pəs) order requiring that a prisoner be brought before a judge or into court to decide whether he or she is being held lawfully. *The right of habeas corpus is a protection against unjust imprisonment.*

**legality** (li gal´ i tē) accordance with the law; lawfulness. *The legality of the constitutional amendment was upheld by the court.*

Name: _____ Date: _____

# Unit 24: Law: *Skills and Practice*

**Directions:** For each word give a **synonym** from the vocabulary word list below. A **synonym** is a word that means the same or nearly the same.

| witness | allegation | evidence | attest | law-abiding |
| legality | penitentiary | culprit | larceny | testimony |

1. facts _____
2. lawfulness _____
3. spectator _____
4. theft _____
5. offender _____
6. testify _____
7. proof _____
8. assertion _____
9. orderly _____
10. prison _____

**Did You Know?** The Babylonians were the first group of people to write down their own laws.

**Directions:** Write an **antonym** from the list of vocabulary words below on the line next to each word. An **antonym** is a word that means the opposite or nearly opposite.

| bungling | objection | legitimate | conviction | defendant | opponent |

1. friend _____
2. approval _____
3. acquittal _____
4. unlawful _____
5. competent _____
6. plaintiff _____

**Directions:** Write a sentence for the following words on your own paper. Remember to check your spelling and punctuation.

| disposition | verdict | subpoena | lawsuit | sequester |
| accomplice | bylaw | summation | habeas corpus | |

**Extend Your Vocabulary**

1. Make a list of famous lawyers.
2. Write the dialogue for a court scene; you make up the crime.
3. Make a list of classroom rules or laws.
4. Interview a lawyer. Publish it in a classroom newspaper.

Name: _____     Date: _____

# Unit 24: Law: *Vocabulary Quiz*

**Directions:** Match each vocabulary word with the correct meaning. Write the word on the line next to the meaning.

| | | | | |
|---|---|---|---|---|
| **bylaw** | **evidence** | **fugitive** | **larceny** | **testimony** |
| **verdict** | **witness** | **objection** | **opponent** | **conviction** |
| **witness** | **allegation** | **subpoena** | **sequester** | **law-abiding** |
| **attest** | **lawsuit** | **accomplice** | **disposition** | **habeas corpus** |
| **culprit** | **defendant** | **legality** | **summation** | **legitimate** |

1. _____ allowed or admitted by law; rightful; lawful

2. _____ statement used for evidence

3. _____ person who knowingly aids another in committing a crime

4. _____ person accused in a court of law

5. _____ order requiring that a prisoner be brought before a judge or into court to decide whether he or she is being held lawfully

6. _____ act of proving or declaring guilty

7. _____ obeying the law; peaceful and orderly

8. _____ the unlawful taking and using of the personal property of another person; theft

9. _____ remove or withdraw from public view

10. _____ an official written order commanding a person to appear in a court of law

11. _____ the final presentation of facts and arguments by the counsel for each side

12. _____ person who is on the other side in a fight, game, or discussion

13. _____ accordance with the law; lawfulness

14. _____ a prison for criminals

15. _____ case in a court of law started by one person to claim something from another

16. _____ anything that shows what is true and what is not; facts; proof

17. _____ a disposing; settlement

18. _____ the decision of a jury

19. _____ person guilty of a fault or crime; offender

20. _____ something said in objecting; reason or argument against something

21. _____ do or make in a clumsy, unskilled way

22. _____ an accusation made without proof

23. _____ person who saw something happen; spectator; eyewitness

24. _____ give proof of; certify; bear witness; testify

25. _____ law made by a city, company, club, and so forth for the control of its own affairs

# Unit 25: Sports

The first <u>modern</u> Olympic Games were held in 1896 in Athens. Thirteen countries competed. A Frenchman, Baron Coubertin, formed the International Olympic Committee in 1894 because he thought sports should be a part of education. This committee still organizes the games and chooses where they will be held. Coubertin is sometimes called the "Father of the Modern Olympic Games" because of his influence.

laurel (lôr´ əl)

international (in´ tər nash´ ə nəl)

champion (cham´ pē ən)

protocol (prōt´ ə kol´)

Olympian (ō lim´ pē ən)

biathlon (bī ath´ lon´)

equestrian (i kwes´ trē ən)

popular (pop´ yə lər)

amateur (am´ ə chər)

hurdles (hûrd´ 'ls)

sprints (sprints)

challenge (chal´ ənj)

commemorative (kə mem´ ə rə tiv´)

marathon (mar´ ə thon´)

javelin (jav´ ə lin)

modern (mod´ ərn)

elite (i lēt´)

luge (loozh)

triathlon (trī ath´ lon´)

qualifying (kwôl´ i fī´ ing)

archery (är´ chər ē)

stamina (stam´ ə nə)

comrade (kom´ rad´)

preliminary (prē lim´ ə ner´ ē)

endurance (en door´ əns)

# Unit 25: Sports: *Get the Facts!*

**laurel** (lôr´ əl) the smooth, shining leaves of a small evergreen tree. *The marathon winner wore a wreath of laurel on his head.*

**marathon** (mar´ ə thon´) a foot race of 26 miles, 385 yards. *He ran the marathon in the Olympics.*

**international** (in´ tər nash´ ə nəl) between or among nations. *The Olympics are international.*

**javelin** (jav´ ə lin) a lightweight spear thrown by hand. *The Olympics still have the javelin throw event today, as they did in ancient times.*

**champion** (cham´ pē ən) person who wins first place in a game or contest. *To get to the Olympics, you must be a champion in your field.*

**modern** (mod´ ərn) present times. *How do the ancient Olympic Games and the modern Olympic Games compare?*

**protocol** (prōt´ ə kol´) rules of etiquette. *The protocol in the opening parade of the Olympics is for the athletes to enter the stadium in alphabetical order of the country's name, except for Greece.*

**elite** (i lēt´) the choice or distinguished part; those thought of as the best people. *Only the elite compete at the Olympics.*

**Olympian** (ō lim´ pē ən) a participant in the Olympic Games. *The Olympian trained for years to win a gold medal in the pole vault.*

**luge (**lo͞ozh) a racing sled for 1 or 2 people that is ridden with the rider or riders lying on their backs. *The luge competition takes place in the Winter Olympics.*

**biathlon** (bī ath´ lon´) a competition that combines cross-country skiing and rifle shooting. *He entered the biathlon competition.*

**triathlon** (trī ath´ lon´) an athletic contest in which participants compete without stopping in three successive events, usually long-distance swimming, biking, and running. *She trained for a long time for the triathlon.*

**equestrian** (i kwes´ trē ən) having to do with horseback riding, horses, or horseback riders. *The American team won the equestrian event at the Olympics.*

**qualifying** (kwôl´ i fī´ ing) make fit or make competent; preparing. *Qualifying is one of the first steps to competing in the Olympics.*

**popular** (pop´ yə lər) liked by most people. *Basketball is a popular team sport at the modern Olympics.*

**archery** (är´ chər ē) practice or sport of shooting with bow and arrow. *Being skillful in archery requires a steady arm and good aim.*

**amateur** (am´ ə chər) person who does something for pleasure, not for money or as a profession. *Amateur athletes from all over the world take part in the Olympic Games.*

**stamina** (stam´ ə nə) strength; endurance. *Olympians need stamina to compete in the events.*

**hurdles** (hûrd´ 'ls) race in which the runners jump over barriers. *She failed to clear two hurdles in her race.*

**comrade** (kom´ rad´) a close companion and friend. *Some Olympians become comrades.*

**sprints** (sprints) race or any short spell of running, rowing, and so on at maximum speed. *He participated in the sprint events because of his top speed.*

**preliminary** (prē lim´ ə ner´ ē) coming before the main business; something preparatory. *The Olympic Committee had many preliminaries before the actual games.*

**challenge** (chal´ ənj) to call to a game or contest. *The athlete accepted the challenge to participate in the race.*

**endurance** (en do͝or´ əns) power to last and to withstand hard wear. *She had great endurance in the swimming event.*

**commemorative** (kə mem´ ə rə tiv´) preserving or honoring the memory of some person or event. *The modern Olympic Games are commemorative of the ancient games.*

Name: _____  Date: _____

# Unit 25: Sports: *Skills and Practice*

**Directions:** For each word give a **synonym** from the vocabulary word list below. A **synonym** is a word that means the same or nearly the same.

| | | | | |
|---|---|---|---|---|
| **champion** | **modern** | **qualifying** | **stamina** | **elite** |
| **Olympian** | **amateur** | **popular** | **comrade** | **laurel** |
| **marathon** | **javelin** | **challenge** | **preliminary** | **luge** |

1. sled _____
2. race _____
3. spear _____
4. leaves _____
5. best _____
6. endurance _____
7. preparatory _____
8. favorite _____
9. training _____
10. participant _____
11. friend _____
12. present _____
13. contend _____
14. novice _____
15. winner _____

**Did You Know?** The first ancient Olympic Games were established in 776 B.C. They were held every four years in Olympia. Problems arose such as paying athletes and bribing judges. These problems brought an end to the ancient Olympic Games. They were not held again for 1500 years.

**Directions:** Write a sentence for the following words on your own paper. Remember to check your spelling and punctuation.

| | | | | |
|---|---|---|---|---|
| **international** | **protocol** | **biathlon** | **endurance** | **hurdles** |
| **commemorative** | **triathlon** | **sprints** | **equestrian** | **archery** |

### Extend Your Vocabulary

1. Compare and contrast the ancient Olympic Games to the modern Olympic Games.
2. Write a narrative piece about your participation in the Olympic Games. How would you feel? Which sport would you choose?
3. Research the Olympic symbol of the five rings. Write about it.
4. Make a list of sports in the summer and winter Olympic Games.

# Unit 25: Sports: *Vocabulary Quiz*

Name: _____   Date: _____

**Directions:** Match each vocabulary word with the correct meaning. Write the word on the line next to the meaning.

| | | | | |
|---|---|---|---|---|
| **international** | **laurel** | **marathon** | **javelin** | **champion** |
| **commemorative** | **elite** | **modern** | **protocol** | **biathlon** |
| **preliminary** | **luge** | **triathlon** | **archery** | **amateur** |
| **endurance** | **sprints** | **stamina** | **hurdles** | **comrade** |
| **challenge** | **Olympian** | **popular** | **equestrian** | **qualifying** |

1. _____ practice or sport of shooting with a bow and arrow

2. _____ the smooth, shining leaves of a small evergreen tree

3. _____ person who wins first place in a game or contest

4. _____ a close companion and friend

5. _____ the choice or distinguished part; those thought of as the best people

6. _____ person who does something for pleasure, not for money or as a profession

7. _____ a lightweight spear thrown by hand

8. _____ coming before the main business; something preparatory

9. _____ having to do with horseback riding, horses, or horseback riders

10. _____ power to last and to withstand hard wear

11. _____ present times

12. _____ strength; endurance

13. _____ a foot race of 26 miles, 385 yards

14. _____ liked by most people

15. _____ rules of etiquette

16. _____ race or any short spell of running, rowing, and so forth at maximum speed

17. _____ a racing sled for 1 or 2 people that is ridden with the rider or riders lying on their backs

18. _____ preserving or honoring the memory of some person or event

19. _____ a competition that combines cross-country skiing and rifle shooting

20. _____ race in which the runners jump over barriers

21. _____ between or among nations

22. _____ to call to a game or contest

23. _____ make fit or make competent; preparing

24. _____ an athletic contest in which participants compete without stopping in three successive events, usually long-distance swimming, biking, and running

25. _____ a participant in the Olympic Games

# Additional Vocabulary Words

abandon
absence
academy
accompany
accomplish
accordion
accurate
accustomed
admiration
advertisement
aisle
allowance
altar
ammunition
annual
apparently
appreciate
arena
ashore

bacteria
ballot
barely
barge
baton
beckon
beech
bellow
beloved
blunder
blur
bough
brim
burden
butler

casket
catalog
cedar
certificate
characteristic
coarse

combination
commission
comparison
congratulate
conscience
corral
correspondent
cultivate
curse

dainty
decay
declaration
definite
demolish
detour
dignity
discourage
distinguish
dominoes
drench

elder
emblem
enable
enchant
establish
eventual
exhaustion
extent

fender
fleece
foreman
forfeit
forge
fret
frisky
fury

galley
gauze

genius
gesture
goddess
gorge
graduate
granite
grub
gully
gypsy

hammock
harpoon
hasty
heed
helm
hinder
homely
household
hustle
hydrogen

imitation
impolite
incident
inform
inherit
instruct
interfere
invade

jagged
judgment

kerosene

lag
lasso
lather
least
leisure
livestock
llama
luxury

maintain
marshmallow
marvel
memorize
merely
miniature
miser
misfortune
mitt
muffle
mutton

naval
nightmare
nuisance

oblige
old-fashioned
oppose
orphanage
outline
overboard

pane
panel
paradise
peacock
permanent
pierce
pliers
porcupine
porridge
prime
prowl

register
rein
remedy
revolver
rove
rubbish
rummage

sapling
scheme
scholar
scroll
sear
shabby
sincerely
sober
sow
squadron
stern
sulphur

thicket
trample
tremendous

vanilla
varnish
vibrate

westward
wit

Name:_____ Date:_____

# Compare and Contrast T-Chart

_____
(Chart Title)

| (Item being compared) | (Item being compared) |
|---|---|
| | |
| | |
| | |
| | |
| | |
| | |
| | |
| | |
| | |
| | |
| | |
| | |
| | |
| | |

\* Use with Extend Your Vocabulary activities asking for a T-chart to compare and contrast two things.

Name:_____ Date:_____

# List Activity

_____

(Title of List)

_____    _____    _____

_____    _____    _____

_____    _____    _____

_____    _____    _____

_____    _____    _____

_____    _____    _____

_____    _____    _____

_____    _____    _____

_____    _____    _____

_____    _____    _____

_____    _____    _____

_____    _____    _____

_____    _____    _____

_____    _____    _____

_____    _____    _____

\* Use with Extend Your Vocabulary activities asking for a list of things.

Name: _____ Date: _____

# Venn Diagram

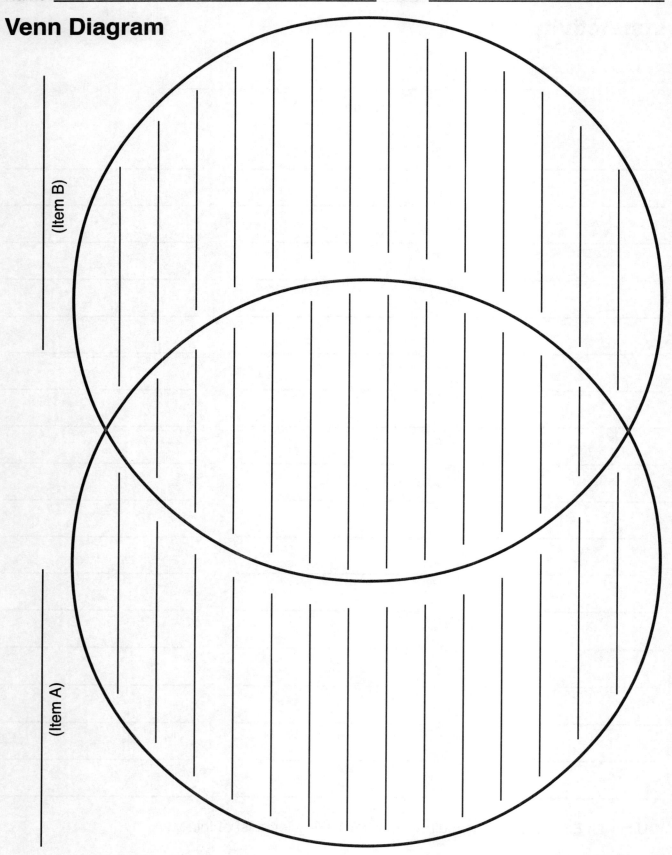

(Item B)

(Item A)

Name: _____     Date: _____

# Vocabulary Variations

**Directions:** Choose a word from your vocabulary list. Write the word on the line, and then fill in as many lines as you can with antonyms and synonyms for the word and different forms of the word.

_____
**(Vocabulary Word)**

| **Antonyms** | **Synonyms** |
| --- | --- |
| _____ | _____ |
| _____ | _____ |
| _____ | _____ |
| _____ | _____ |
| _____ | _____ |
| _____ | _____ |
| _____ | _____ |

**Word Forms**

_____

_____

_____

_____

_____

_____

_____

Name:_____ Date:_____

# Word Web

**Directions:** Choose a word from your vocabulary list. Write the word in the center. Fill in the rest of the word web.

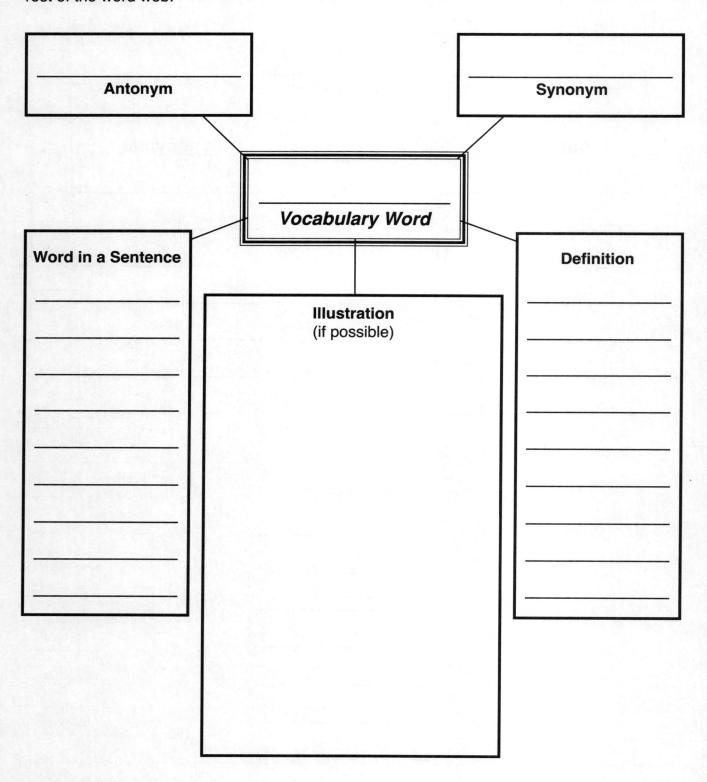

Name: _____ Date: _____

# Word Search

**Directions:** Use your vocabulary words to make your own word search. Give it to a partner to try when you are finished. Write the list of words below the puzzle for your partner to use when finding the words.

_____ _____ _____ _____

_____ _____ _____ _____

_____ _____ _____ _____

_____ _____ _____ _____

_____ _____ _____ _____

Name:_____     Date:_____

# Vocabulary ABC

**Directions:** Choose a word from your vocabulary list. Try to find 26 new words that are related to that word and begin with a different letter of the alphabet. Check your spelling.

**Vocabulary word:** _____

A _____     N _____

B _____     O _____

C _____     P _____

D _____     Q _____

E _____     R _____

F _____     S _____

G _____     T _____

H _____     U _____

I _____     V _____

J _____     W _____

K _____     X _____

L _____     Y _____

M _____     Z _____

Name:_____ Date:_____

# Author Time!

**Directions:** Compose a writing piece using as many words from your vocabulary list as you can. Keep in mind your list of words and the many types of writing you could do, such as persuasive, expository, or narrative. Use extra paper if you need it.

List your vocabulary words. Place an X by the ones you use in your writing piece.

_____   _____   _____   _____
_____   _____   _____   _____
_____   _____   _____   _____
_____   _____   _____   _____
_____   _____   _____   _____

Writing piece:

_____
_____
_____
_____
_____
_____
_____
_____
_____
_____
_____
_____
_____
_____
_____
_____

Name: _____ Date: _____

# Student Self-Evaluation Form

**Directions:** Place a check mark in the box next to the best answer.

1. I studied my vocabulary words.

   ☐ yes        ☐ some        ☐ no

2. I understood the meanings of my vocabulary words.

   ☐ yes        ☐ some        ☐ no

3. I could pronounce my vocabulary words.

   ☐ yes        ☐ some        ☐ no

4. I proofread for spelling errors in my writing.

   ☐ yes        ☐ sometimes        ☐ not yet

5. I did well on my vocabulary activities.

   ☐ yes        ☐ sometimes        ☐ no

6. I used vocabulary resources, such as dictionaries, thesauruses, word lists, and so on.

   ☐ yes        ☐ sometimes        ☐ not yet

I am going to work next on _____

_____

_____

Comments _____

_____

_____

_____

_____

# Teacher Notes

_____

_____

_____

_____

_____

_____

_____

_____

_____

_____

_____

_____

_____

_____

_____

_____

_____

_____

---

Name: _____     Date: _____

## Unit 1: Africa: *Skills and Practice*

**Directions:** For each word give a **synonym** from the vocabulary word list below. A **synonym** is a word that means the same or nearly the same.

| | | | | |
|---|---|---|---|---|
| lute | kente | mancala | gourd | headdress |
| thatch | ivory | soapstone | kudu | sanctions |
| okapi | integral | terra cotta | boycott | |

1. straw _thatch_
2. necessary _integral_
3. instrument _lute_
4. mammal _okapi_
5. antelope _kudu_
6. cloth _kente_
7. rock _soapstone_
8. game _mancala_
9. clay _terra cotta_
10. squash _gourd_
11. tusks _ivory_
12. gele _headdress_
13. protest _boycott_
     _sanctions_

> **Did You Know?** Clapping was a gesture of thanks when receiving a gift in Africa; and no matter how small the gift, it was received with both hands. This symbolized that it was a generous give.

**Directions:** Write a sentence for the following words on your own paper. Remember to check your spelling and punctuation.

| | | | |
|---|---|---|---|
| missionary | equatorial | rift valley | rapids | semiarid |
| preserves | Pygmy | loom | apartheid | kraal |
| imperialism | | | | |

**Extend Your Vocabulary**

1. Make a list of all of the African countries.
2. Compare and contrast two countries in Africa; include things such as customs and religion.
3. Research the importance of the Nile River.
4. Make a ceremonial African mask. Use a variety of materials.

   3

---

Name: _____     Date: _____

## Unit 1: Africa: *Vocabulary Quiz*

**Directions:** Match each vocabulary word with the correct meaning. Write the word on the line next to the meaning.

| | | | | |
|---|---|---|---|---|
| equatorial | rift valley | rapids | semiarid | preserve |
| lute | okapi | Pygmy | imperialism | missionary |
| boycott | apartheid | sanctions | loom | kente |
| integral | thatch | gourd | kraal | headdress |
| ivory | terra cotta | kudu | mancala | soapstone |

1. _thatch_ straw or palm leaves, for example, used as a roof or covering
2. _rift valley_ a long, steep-sided valley lying between two parallel faults
3. _sanctions_ actions such as boycotts taken by one or more countries to keep certain benefits from another country
4. _rapids_ part of a river's course where the water rushes quickly, often over rocks near the surface
5. _headdress_ covering or decoration for the head
6. _okapi_ an African mammal that is related to the giraffe but is smaller, without spots, and has a much shorter neck
7. _loom_ a machine for weaving thread into cloth
8. _equatorial_ of, at, or near the equator
9. _terra cotta_ kind of hard, brownish-red earthenware used for statues or vases
10. _imperialism_ the extension of a country's power over other lands by military, political, or economic means
11. _kente_ a brightly colored cloth woven by the Asante and Ewe peoples
12. _semiarid_ having very little rainfall
13. _kudu_ a large, grayish-brown African antelope with white stripes
14. _boycott_ a special kind of protest when a group of people refuse to buy or use goods produced by another group
15. _integral_ necessary to make something complete; essential
16. _preserve_ a place where wild animals, fish, trees, or plants are protected
17. _kraal_ a South African village, usually surrounded by a stockade; a fenced pen for cattle or sheep
18. _lute_ a musical instrument having a pear-shaped body with six pairs of strings
19. _gourd_ any of various fleshy fruits that grow on vines and are related to squash
20. _missionary_ a person who tries to spread his or her religion to others with different beliefs
21. _mancala_ an African game
22. _apartheid_ a policy of South African government that was designed to keep the races separate and unequal
23. _ivory_ a hard, white substance of which tusks of elephants or walruses are composed
24. _Pygmy_ one of a group of people of Africa who are less than five feet tall
25. _soapstone_ a soft rock that feels like soap

   4

---

Name: _____     Date: _____

## Unit 2: Mysteries: *Skills and Practice*

**Directions:** For each word give a **synonym** from the vocabulary word list below. A **synonym** is a word that means the same or nearly the same.

| | | | | |
|---|---|---|---|---|
| aloof | clue | fugitive | deduction | testimony |
| sleuth | witness | admonition | hypothesis | ciphers |
| appraise | analyzing | purloin | sinister | hearsay |

1. hint _clue_
2. inference _deduction_
3. detective _sleuth_
4. warning _admonition_
5. evil _sinister_
6. codes _ciphers_
7. theory _hypothesis_
8. examining _analyzing_
9. estimate _appraise_
10. rumor _hearsay_
11. steal _purloin_
12. indifferent _aloof_
13. runaway _fugitive_
14. deposition _testimony_
15. observer _witness_

> **Did You Know?** The first Sherlock Homes mystery, *A Study in Scarlet*, written by Sir Arthur Conan Doyle, was published in 1887. It was so successful that Doyle gave up his medical practice to write full-time.

**Directions:** Write an **antonym** from the list of vocabulary words below on the line next to each word. An **antonym** is a word that means the opposite or nearly opposite.

| | |
|---|---|
| breakthrough | disclosure |

1. concealment _disclosure_
2. problem _breakthrough_

**Directions:** Write a sentence for the following words on your own paper. Remember to check your spelling and punctuation.

| | | | |
|---|---|---|---|
| alibi | red herring | suspects | newsmonger |
| hunch | eavesdropper | strategies | disguise |

**Extend Your Vocabulary**

1. Hide an object in the classroom. Make a list of clues for a classmate to locate the object.
2. Make a list of famous detectives.
3. Imagine that you are at the scene of a crime. Write about what you might hear, smell, or see.
4. As a class, research a famous mystery author. Write a report about him or her.

   7

---

Name: _____     Date: _____

## Unit 2: Mysteries: *Vocabulary Quiz*

**Directions:** Match each vocabulary word with the correct meaning. Write the word on the line next to the meaning.

| | | | | |
|---|---|---|---|---|
| alibi | clue | deduction | sinister | red herring |
| sleuth | suspects | witness | ciphers | disguise |
| analyzing | strategies | fugitive | appraise | hypothesis |
| testimony | eavesdropper | newsmonger | admonition | breakthrough |
| hearsay | purloin | disclosure | aloof | hunch |

1. _testimony_ statement used for evidence or proof
2. _alibi_ a suspect's claim that he or she was not near the crime scene at the time of the crime
3. _hypothesis_ something assumed because it seems likely to be a true explanation; theory
4. _witness_ the person who discovers a crime or has some kind of information about the crime
5. _disclosure_ something disclosed; open to view; made known
6. _ciphers_ secret writings; codes
7. _appraise_ estimate the value or amount
8. _red herring_ false clue that misleads a detective in an investigation
9. _admonition_ gentle reproof or warning
10. _suspects_ the people who are connected to the crime in some way and appear to have a motive for committing the crime
11. _eavesdropper_ person who listens to talk he or she is not supposed to hear or listens secretly to a private conversation
12. _clue_ something that appears to lead the detective closer to solving the crime, mystery, or problem
13. _hearsay_ common talk; gossip or rumor
14. _disguise_ use of changes in clothes or appearance to hide who one really is or to look like someone else
15. _hunch_ vague feeling of suspicion
16. _strategies_ skillful planning and management of anything
17. _newsmonger_ a gossip
18. _deduction_ using the facts to infer a conclusion; inference
19. _breakthrough_ solution of some baffling problem
20. _sleuth_ detective
21. _aloof_ indifferent; reserved; tending to keep to oneself
22. _sinister_ bad; evil; dishonest
23. _purloin_ steal
24. _analyzing_ examining carefully and in detail
25. _fugitive_ person who is running away or who has run away

   8

---

## Unit 3: Family: Skills and Practice

**Directions:** For each word give a **synonym** from the vocabulary word list below. A **synonym** is a word that means the same or nearly the same.

| matrimony | lineage | spouse | offspring | accommodating |
| sibling | kindred | mutual | commitment | reconciliation |
| alliance | | | | |

1. marriage _matrimony_  2. wife _spouse_
3. promise _commitment_  4. ancestry _lineage_
5. brother _sibling_  6. obliging _accommodating_
7. related _kindred_  8. same _mutual_
9. forgiveness _reconciliation_  10. union _alliance_
11. litter _offspring_

**Did You Know?** On January 6, French families eat a special dinner together. The children eat slices of a flat almond pie called a *galette*. A charm is hidden in one of the slices. Whoever finds the charm is crowned king or queen for the night.

**Directions:** Write an **antonym** from the list of vocabulary words below on the line next to each word. An **antonym** is a word that means the opposite or nearly opposite.

| nourishing | domestic | continuous | compatible |

1. disagreeing _compatible_  2. starving _nourishing_
3. broken _continuous_  4. wild _domestic_

**Directions:** Write a sentence for the following words on your own paper. Remember to check your spelling and punctuation.

| generation | reunion | parentage | complementary | race |
| congenial | genealogy | reciprocal | fraternity | |

**Extend Your Vocabulary**

1. Research your family genealogy and make a family tree.
2. Write a narrative piece about a reunion you have attended.
3. Write a persuasive piece about why it is better to be the oldest, middle, or youngest child in your family.
4. Make a list of ways to be compatible with your siblings.

© Mark Twain Media, Inc., Publishers  11

## Unit 3: Family: Vocabulary Quiz

**Directions:** Match each vocabulary word with the correct meaning. Write the word on the line next to the meaning.

| compatible | domestic | matrimony | spouse | generation |
| reunion | offspring | commitment | ancestry | lineage |
| parentage | alliance | sibling | fraternity | kindred |
| mutual | nourishing | genealogy | congenial | complementary |
| reconciliation | reciprocal | race | continuous | accommodating |

1. _accommodating_ willing to do favors; obliging
2. _domestic_ of the home, household, or family affairs
3. _fraternity_ group having the same interests or kind of work; brotherhood
4. _offspring_ the young of a person, animal, or plant; descendant
5. _nourishing_ keeping well-fed and healthy
6. _parentage_ descent from parents; family line
7. _continuous_ without a stop or break; connected; unbroken
8. _sibling_ brother or sister
9. _mutual_ done felt, or said by one toward the other; shared in common
10. _matrimony_ marriage
11. _congenial_ having similar tastes and interests; getting on well together
12. _commitment_ a pledge; promise
13. _reconciliation_ settlement or adjustment of disagreements or differences
14. _spouse_ husband or wife
15. _kindred_ like; similar; related
16. _compatible_ able to exist or get along well together; in agreement
17. _reciprocal_ in return
18. _ancestry_ line of descent from ancestors; lineage
19. _race_ persons, animals, or plants having the same ancestors
20. _alliance_ a union of persons or groups formed by agreement for some special purpose
21. _complementary_ completing or making perfect
22. _generation_ all the people born at about the same time
23. _genealogy_ account of the descent of a person or family from an ancestor
24. _reunion_ a social gathering of persons who have been separated or who have interests in common
25. _lineage_ descent in a direct line from an ancestor

© Mark Twain Media, Inc., Publishers  12

## Unit 4: Business: Skills and Practice

**Directions:** For each word give a **synonym** from the vocabulary word list below. A **synonym** is a word that means the same or nearly the same.

| pursuit | agenda | negotiation | inventory | barter |
| vendor | errand | merger | portfolio | interchange |

1. trade _barter_  2. stock _inventory_
3. arrangement _negotiation_  4. occupation _pursuit_
5. seller _vendor_  6. exchange _interchange_
7. briefcase _portfolio_  8. consolidation _merger_
9. syllabus _agenda_  10. task _errand_

**Did You Know?** James Ritty was the inventor of the cash register. He invented it in 1879 for his saloon in Ohio.

**Directions:** Write an **antonym** from the list of vocabulary words below on the line next to each word. An **antonym** is a word that means the opposite or nearly opposite.

| bankrupt | employee | monopoly | retail |

1. wholesale _retail_  2. employer _employee_
3. solvent _bankrupt_  4. free trade _monopoly_

**Directions:** Write a sentence for the following words on your own paper. Remember to check your spelling and punctuation.

| commerce | franchise | monopoly | transaction | Rolodex |
| broker | maneuver | workmanship | enterprise | payroll |

**Extend Your Vocabulary**

1. Set up a make-believe business. Tell about the details such as supplies, location, jobs, employees, and so on.
2. Make a list of franchises. Research the number one franchise in the United States.
3. Make a monthly expense account on how you spend your allowance. Record all expenses.
4. Make a list of the different people who use a portfolio.

© Mark Twain Media, Inc., Publishers  15

## Unit 4: Business: Vocabulary Quiz

**Directions:** Match each vocabulary word with the correct meaning. Write the word on the line next to the meaning.

| barter | commerce | franchise | inventory | merger |
| monopoly | transaction | vendor | bankrupt | pursuit |
| agenda | errand | portfolio | broker | negotiation |
| employee | interchange | wholesale | retail | maneuver |
| workmanship | enterprise | payroll | ledger | Rolodex |

1. _broker_ person who buys and sells stocks, bonds, and securities for other people
2. _inventory_ all the articles listed or to be listed; stock
3. _retail_ sale of goods in small quantities directly to the consumer
4. _vendor_ seller; peddler
5. _payroll_ list of persons to be paid and the amount that each one is to receive
6. _errand_ what one is sent to do
7. _negotiation_ an arrangement
8. _barter_ to trade by exchanging one kind of goods for other goods without using money
9. _wholesale_ sale of goods in large quantities at a time, usually to those who will, in turn, sell them to consumers
10. _commerce_ the buying and selling of goods between different places, especially in large amounts
11. _employee_ person who works for another person or firm for pay
12. _merger_ combination; consolidation
13. _workmanship_ the art or skill of a worker or the work done
14. _pursuit_ that which one does as a profession, recreation, or occupation
15. _Rolodex_ a trademark for an item that functions as a desktop rotary file of removable cards for names, addresses, and telephone numbers
16. _franchise_ privilege of selling the products of a manufacturer in a given area
17. _interchange_ give and take; exchange
18. _agenda_ list of things to be dealt with or done
19. _maneuver_ a skillful plan or movement
20. _monopoly_ the exclusive control of a commodity or service
21. _enterprise_ an undertaking or project
22. _portfolio_ a portable case for carrying loose papers; briefcase
23. _ledger_ book of accounts in which a business keeps a record of all money transactions
24. _bankrupt_ unable to pay one's debts
25. _transaction_ piece of business

© Mark Twain Media, Inc., Publishers  16

---

## Unit 5: World War II: *Skills and Practice*

Name: _____ Date: _____

**Directions:** For each word give a **synonym** from the vocabulary word list below. A **synonym** is a word that means the same or nearly the same.

| atom bomb | blitzkrieg | pogrom | compensation |
|-----------|-----------|--------|--------------|
| Swastika | atrocity | sabotage | |

1. pay *compensation*
2. massacre *pogrom*
3. Nazi emblem *swastika*
4. weapon *atom bomb*
5. cruelty *atrocity*
6. damage *sabotage*
7. attack *blitzkrieg*

> **Did You Know?** Adolf Hitler succeeded in killing two-thirds of all Jews in Europe before he ended his own life in his bomb-proof bunker under the German Chancellery in Berlin at the end of war.

**Directions:** Write an **antonym** from the list of vocabulary words below on the line next to each word. An **antonym** is a word that means the opposite or nearly opposite.

| extermination | optimistic | allies | deportation |
|---------------|-----------|--------|-------------|

1. pessimistic *optimistic*
2. remain *deportation*
3. create *extermination*
4. enemies *allies*

**Directions:** Write a sentence for the following words on your own paper. Remember to check your spelling and punctuation.

| concentration camp | Holocaust | relocation | riveter | Nazi |
|--------------------|-----------|-----------|---------|------|
| anti-Semitism | rationing | scapegoat | ghetto | Axis |
| home front | Resistance | economic | | |

**Extend Your Vocabulary**

1. Compare and contrast the causes for World War I and World War II.
2. Research Anne Frank and her role in World War II. Write a report about her.
3. Research Japanese relocation camps. Write a mini-report.
4. Explore World War II through music by listing to the popular songs of that time. How do they reflect the spirit of the people?

19

---

## Unit 5: World War II: *Vocabulary Quiz*

Name: _____ Date: _____

**Directions:** Match each vocabulary word with the correct meaning. Write the word on the line next to the meaning.

| relocation | blitzkrieg | Holocaust | concentration camp | Allies |
|-----------|-----------|-----------|--------------------|--------|
| Axis | Nazi | Resistance | compensation | atom bomb |
| swastika | deportation | ghetto | pogrom | home front |
| rationing | optimistic | pessimistic | anti-Semitism | riveter |
| scapegoat | economic | sabotage | extermination | atrocity |

1. *rationing* to allow only certain amounts of food, gasoline, and other goods to each person
2. *relocation* move to a new place; locate or settle anew
3. *concentration camp* prison camps established by Adolf Hitler and the Nazi Party for Jews and other political prisoners during World War II
4. *Axis* the alliance of Germany, Italy, and Japan
5. *economic* having to do with economics, the science of production, distribution, and consumption of goods and services
6. *atom bomb* powerful weapon created from the splitting of atoms
7. *optimistic* hoping for the best; inclined to look on the bright side of things
8. *compensation* something given to make up for something else
9. *extermination* complete destruction
10. *ghetto* part of a city in Europe where Jews were required to live
11. *home front* term given to the U.S. mainland during the war
12. *blitzkrieg* sudden, violent attack using many airplanes and tanks
13. *pogrom* an organized massacre of helpless people
14. *Resistance* people who secretly organize and fight for their freedom in a country occupied and controlled by a foreign power
15. *pessimistic* inclined to look on the dark side of things; to see all the difficulties and disadvantages
16. *Allies* countries fighting along with the United States against the Axis powers
17. *riveter* person in a factory that makes or fastens with rivets
18. *Holocaust* mass murder of European Jews by Adolf Hitler and the Nazis
19. *sabotage* damage done by enemy agents or by civilians of a conquered nation
20. *Nazi* member of the German political party called the National Socialist German Workers Party
21. *anti-Semitism* dislike or hatred for Jews; prejudice against Jews
22. *swastika* emblem on the Nazi flag
23. *scapegoat* person or thing made to bear the blame for the mistakes or sins of others
24. *deportation* removal from a country by banishment or expulsion
25. *atrocity* very great wickedness or cruelty

20

---

## Unit 6: Ecology: *Skills and Practice*

Name: _____ Date: _____

**Directions:** Write a **synonym** from the list of vocabulary words below on the line. A **synonym** is a word that means the same or nearly the same.

| noxious | woodland | conservation | camouflage |
|---------|----------|--------------|------------|
| temperate | grassland | endangered | bivouac |

1. disguise *camouflage*
2. poisonous *noxious*
3. camp *bivouac*
4. jeopardy *endangered*
5. mild *temperate*
6. forest *woodland*
7. savanna *grassland*
8. preservation *conservation*

> **Did You Know?** Julius Sterling Morton was responsible for establishing the first Arbor Day in the United States. Arbor Day is a day set aside for planting trees.

**Directions:** Fill in each blank with the correct vocabulary word from below.

| dust bowl | ozone layer | deciduous | coniferous |
|-----------|-------------|-----------|------------|
| deforestation | species | | |

1. pines *coniferous*
2. shield of air *ozone*
3. western plains *dust bowl*
4. maples, elms *deciduous*
5. animals *species*
6. tree removal *deforestation*

**Directions:** Write a sentence for each of the vocabulary words below on your own paper. Remember to check for spelling and punctuation.

| biome | ecosystem | tundra | broad-leaved | bract |
|-------|-----------|--------|--------------|-------|
| humus | mammalogy | canopy | understory | aerate |

**Extend Your Vocabulary**

1. Make a list of ways you can recycle.
2. Research the food chain and make a drawing of a food chain you are a part of.
3. Choose an endangered species. Write a report.
4. Read as a class, *50 Simple Things Kids Can Do to Save the Earth*. Write a reaction.

23

---

## Unit 6: Ecology: *Vocabulary Quiz*

Name: _____ Date: _____

**Directions:** Match each vocabulary word with the correct meaning. Write the word on the line next to the meaning.

| biome | ecosystem | coniferous | deciduous | humus |
|-------|-----------|-----------|-----------|-------|
| savanna | grassland | tundra | temperate | bract |
| woodland | broad-leaved | mammalogy | conservation | ozone layer |
| endangered | dust bowl | species | deforestation | canopy |
| camouflage | understory | noxious | bivouac | aerate |

1. *understory* layer that consists of the tops of smaller trees, which receive less light than the canopy
2. *savanna* a grassy plain with few or no trees
3. *dust bowl* area in the western plains of the United States and Canada where dust storms are frequent and violent
4. *broad-leaved* having broad leaves; leaves that are not needles
5. *canopy* green and leafy layer in the rain forest 80–150 feet above the ground, where large, broad leaves catch and block both rain and sunlight
6. *biome* a large geographical area having generally the same climate and vegetation
7. *noxious* very harmful; poisonous
8. *mammalogy* branch of zoology dealing with mammals
9. *bract* a small leaf growing at the base of a flower or flower stalk
10. *deciduous* shedding leaves each year
11. *endangered* brought into danger or peril
12. *ecosystem* a community of interlocking parts that act upon each other in life's grand plan
13. *camouflage* a disguise or false appearance for the purpose of concealing
14. *humus* a dark-brown or black part of soil formed from decayed leaves and other vegetable matter
15. *ozone* a protective shield of air high up in the earth's atmosphere
16. *conservation* a preserving from harm or decay; protection from loss
17. *species* groups of animals or plants that have certain permanent characteristics in common and are able to interbreed
18. *coniferous* bearing cones
19. *deforestation* removal of trees
20. *woodland* land covered with trees
21. *bivouac* camp outdoors, usually without tents or with very small tents
22. *grassland* land with grass on it, used for pasture
23. *aerate* expose to and mix with air
24. *temperate* not very hot and not very cold
25. *tundra* a vast, level, treeless plain in the arctic regions

24

---

Name: _____ Date: _____

## Unit 7: Space: *Skills and Practice*

**Directions:** Categorize each of the vocabulary words below and write the word on the line under the correct category. Some words may be used more than once.

| | | | | |
|---|---|---|---|---|
| sunspot | lunar | galaxy | interplanetary | corona |
| nebula | orbit | equinox | constellation | eclipse |
| solstice | asteroid | supernova | | |

**Stars**
- supernova
- constellation
- nebula
- galaxy

**Sun**
- sunspot
- corona
- eclipse
- solstice
- equinox

**Planets**
- orbit
- interplanetary
- asteroid

**Moon**
- lunar
- eclipse

> **Did You Know?** The record for the longest comet tail was the Great Comet of 1843. Its tail stretched 200 million miles!

**Directions:** Write a sentence for the following words on your own paper. Remember to check your spelling and punctuation.

| | | | | |
|---|---|---|---|---|
| celestial | astronomy | cosmos | galaxy | ever-expanding |
| planetarium | black hole | astronomer | gravity | satellite |

### Extend Your Vocabulary
1. Research the order of the planets and illustrate them in a diagram. Label the planets.
2. Pick a planet and write a report on it.
3. Make a list of celestial bodies.
4. Write a report about a planetarium and include the things you do there. Visit one if possible.

---

Name: _____ Date: _____

## Unit 7: Space: *Vocabulary Quiz*

**Directions:** Match each vocabulary word with the correct meaning. Write the word on the line next to the meaning.

| | | | | |
|---|---|---|---|---|
| eclipse | lunar | constellation | celestial | interplanetary |
| asteroid | cosmos | astronomy | sunspot | ever-expanding |
| equinox | comet | planetarium | black hole | astronomer |
| aurora | satellite | orbit | corona | gravity |
| nebula | supernova | galaxy | quasars | solstice |

1. **orbit** curved, usually somewhat oval path of a heavenly body, planet, or satellite about another body in space
2. **lunar** of the moon, like the moon
3. **astronomer** one who is skilled in astronomy
4. **asteroid** any of thousands of very small planets that revolve about the sun; planetoid
5. **gravity** the natural force that causes objects to move or tend to move toward the center of the earth
6. **ever-expanding** increasing or growing larger indefinitely
7. **solstice** a point in Earth's orbit around the sun where daylight is either the longest or shortest amount possible
8. **black hole** an invisible object in space with mass and gravitational force that is so strong that even light is unable to escape from it
9. **corona** a crown of glowing gases seen around the sun
10. **celestial** of the sky or the heavens
11. **aurora** the display of lights in the near polar latitudes
12. **eclipse** a complete or partial blocking of light passing from one heavenly body to another
13. **nebula** cloud of gas and dust in space
14. **astronomy** science that deals with the sun, moon, planets, stars, and other heavenly bodies
15. **sunspot** one of the dark spots that appear on the surface of the sun
16. **equinox** a point in Earth's orbit around the sun where nights and days are the same length
17. **planetarium** building that has an apparatus that shows the movement of the sun, moon, planets, and stars by projecting lights onto the inside of a dome
18. **supernova** the explosion of a star
19. **cosmos** the universe as thought of as an orderly, harmonious system
20. **satellite** an artificial object launched by rockets into an orbit around the earth or a heavenly body
21. **constellation** group of stars usually having a recognized shape
22. **galaxy** a system of billions of stars, gases, and dust
23. **interplanetary** situated or taking place between planets
24. **quasars** very bright objects in space that may be the powerhouses of developing galaxies
25. **comet** a small, frozen mass of dust and gas revolving around the sun

---

Name: _____ Date: _____

## Unit 8: Immigration: *Skills and Practice*

**Directions:** Write a **synonym** from the list of vocabulary words below on the line next to each word. A **synonym** is a word that means the same or nearly the same.

| | | | | |
|---|---|---|---|---|
| heritage | moor | swindler | persecuted | fiesta |
| custom | treasured | stowage | famine | |

1. hunger   famine
2. cheater   swindler
3. valued   treasured
4. festival   fiesta
5. secure   moor
6. storage   stowage
7. oppressed   persecuted
8. inheritance   heritage
9. habit   custom

> **Did You Know?** Immigrants brought musical traditions from their homelands. The opera came from Italy; symphonies came from Russia; and calypso came from the Caribbean.

**Directions:** Write an **antonym** from the list of vocabulary words below on the line next to each word. An **antonym** is a word that means the opposite or nearly opposite.

| | | | |
|---|---|---|---|
| wayworn | slang | realize | choice |
| | lure | | |

1. misunderstood   realize
2. repel   lure
3. active   wayworn
4. mandate   choice
5. formal   slang

**Directions:** Write a sentence for the following words on your own paper. Remember to check your spelling and punctuation.

| | | | | |
|---|---|---|---|---|
| manifest | bilingual | chopsticks | indentured | steerage |
| melting pot | surname | patronymic | naturalization | ethnic |
| homeland | | | | |

### Extend Your Vocabulary
1. Pretend you're an immigrant child. Write a diary entry of a day on the ship. How did you feel?
2. Make a list of things you treasure.
3. Read the book, *If Your Name Was Changed at Ellis Island.* Write a reaction.
4. Research different groups of immigrants who came to the United States, and make a time line of the different groups' arrivals.

---

Name: _____ Date: _____

## Unit 8: Immigration: *Vocabulary Quiz*

**Directions:** Match each vocabulary word with the correct meaning. Write the word on the line next to the meaning.

| | | | | |
|---|---|---|---|---|
| swindler | indentured | steerage | melting pot | surname |
| patronymic | naturalization | fiesta | persecuted | ethnic |
| famine | treasured | slang | heritage | homeland |
| custom | stowage | moor | manifest | bilingual |
| chopsticks | realize | choice | lure | wayworn |

1. **wayworn** wearied by traveling
2. **melting pot** a place exhibiting racial uniting and absorbing into the cultural tradition of a group or population
3. **bilingual** able to speak another language as well as one's own; knowing two languages
4. **heritage** what is handed down from one generation to the next; inheritance
5. **chopsticks** pair of small, slender sticks used by the Chinese and Japanese to raise food to the mouth
6. **indentured** bound by a contract to serve someone else
7. **custom** any usual action or practice; habit; a long-established habit having the force of law
8. **naturalization** foreigner being admitted to citizenship
9. **homeland** country that is one's home
10. **ethnic** of people of foreign birth or descent
11. **moor** fix firmly; secure; tie down or anchor a ship
12. **swindler** person who cheats or defrauds
13. **treasured** valuable; much loved or valued
14. **surname** last name; family name
15. **choice** act of picking out; selecting from a number of items
16. **persecuted** treated badly; harmed again and again; oppressed
17. **stowage** place or receptacle for storage; storage
18. **steerage** the part of a passenger ship occupied by passengers traveling at the cheapest rate
19. **realize** to make real; achieve; be fully aware of
20. **patronymic** derived from the name of the father or a paternal ancestor
21. **lure** power of attracting or fascinating; charm; attraction
22. **famine** lack of food in a place; a time of starving
23. **manifest** an itemized list of cargo or passengers on a ship
24. **fiesta** festivity; festival
25. **slang** words, phrases, or meanings, etc., not accepted as proper English

---

## Unit 9: Ancient Civilizations: *Skills and Practice*

**Directions:** For each word give a **synonym** from the vocabulary word list below. A **synonym** is a word that means the same or nearly the same.

| proverb | pharaoh | citadel | tributary |
|---|---|---|---|
| scribe | ziggurat | Hebrew | oracle |

1. fortress _Citadel_
2. temple _ziggurat_
3. stream _tributary_
4. Jew _Hebrew_
5. priest _oracle_
6. adage _proverb_
7. writer _scribe_
8. Egyptian ruler _pharaoh_

**Did You Know?** There were approximately 50 million people in the Roman Empire; it covered countries from Britain to Africa. Because of this, the empire had different climates. The Romans suffered from the extremely hot summer temperatures in Egypt, while others shivered in the Swiss Alps and Northern Britain.

**Directions:** Write an **antonym** from the list of vocabulary words below on the line next to each word. An **antonym** is a word that means the opposite or nearly opposite.

| migration | flourish | irrigation | monotheism |
|---|---|---|---|

1. polytheism _monotheism_
2. wither _flourish_
3. drought _irrigation_
4. stability _migration_

**Directions:** Write a sentence for the following words on your own paper. Remember to check your spelling and punctuation.

| papyrus | hieroglyphics | pyramid | ibis | cuneiform |
|---|---|---|---|---|
| Judaism | subcontinent | dynasty | silt | ankh |
| charioteer | | | | |

**Extend Your Vocabulary**

1. Find a website on the Internet on hieroglyphics. Print out your name in hieroglyphics.
2. Research a pyramid. Divide the class into three groups. Make pyramids out of three different types of material.
3. Find three proverbs and write them on a sheet of paper. Explain what they actually mean.
4. Research King Tutankhamun. Write a persuasive piece about his death: murder or not?

## Unit 9: Ancient Civilizations: *Vocabulary Quiz*

**Directions:** Match each vocabulary word with the correct meaning. Write the word on the line next to the meaning.

| scribe | papyrus | hieroglyphics | pyramid | pharaoh |
|---|---|---|---|---|
| ankh | ibis | ziggurat | cuneiform | Judaism |
| polytheism | monotheism | subcontinent | citadel | dynasty |
| oracle | flourish | Hebrew | proverb | irrigation |
| silt | charioteer | empire | migration | tributary |

1. _dynasty_ a line of rulers who belong to the same family and pass control from one generation to the next
2. _pyramid_ huge stone structure built by the ancient Egyptians as a royal tomb
3. _irrigation_ the watering of dry land by means of streams, canals, or pipes in order to grow more crops
4. _ziggurat_ a large temple built by ancient Sumerians
5. _oracle_ a special priest in ancient Chinese society who was believed to receive messages from the gods
6. _scribe_ person who copies manuscripts
7. _silt_ bits of black soil, sand, and clay laid down by flowing water
8. _Judaism_ a world religion founded by the ancient Hebrews
9. _migration_ the movement of a large group of people from one country or region to another in order to settle there
10. _ankh_ an ancient Egyptian symbol of life, a cross with a loop on top
11. _Citadel_ a walled-in area, similar to a fortress, built to protect a city
12. _hieroglyphics_ a system of writing in ancient Egypt
13. _Hebrew_ Jew; Israelite
14. _Cuneiform_ a system of writing developed in ancient Sumeria
15. _charioteer_ person who drives a chariot
16. _monotheism_ belief in one god
17. _empire_ a group of lands and people under one government
18. _ibis_ a large, long-legged wading bird of warm regions, having a long, downward-curving bill
19. _flourish_ grow or develop with vigor; do well; thrive
20. _pharaoh_ the supreme ruler of ancient Egypt
21. _proverb_ a short, wise saying used for a long time by many people
22. _papyrus_ a type of paper made from reeds
23. _subcontinent_ a large land mass that is connected to a continent
24. _tributary_ a small river or stream that flows into a large river
25. _polytheism_ belief in many gods

## Unit 10: Wishes and Dreams: *Skills and Practice*

**Directions:** Write a **synonym** from the list of vocabulary words below on the line next to each word. A **synonym** is a word that means the same or nearly the same.

| desire | mirage | enviable | wistful | inclination |
|---|---|---|---|---|
| ambition | yearn | hankering | trance | anticipate |
| intention | visionary | ponder | abstract | |

1. illusion _mirage_
2. preference _inclination_
3. craving _hankering_
4. expect _anticipate_
5. dreamer _visionary_
6. consider _ponder_
7. purpose _intention_
8. unconsciousness _trance_
9. unreal _abstract_
10. goal _ambition_
11. longing _desire_ _wistful_ _yearn_
12. worthy _enviable_

**Did You Know?** The origin of dream interpretation is unknown. Some of the earliest examples of dreams being interpreted were in the Bible.

**Directions:** Write a sentence for the following words on your own paper. Remember to check your spelling and punctuation.

| aspire | covet | cherish | inspiration | imagery | expectation |
|---|---|---|---|---|---|
| delusion | whimsy | figment | idealize | | |

**Extend Your Vocabulary**

1. Write about one of your dreams. Try to explain what it means.
2. If you had three wishes, what would they be and why? Write about it.
3. Make a list of visionaries in the history of the United States.
4. What are some things you have a hankering for? Compare your list with a classmate's.

## Unit 10: Wishes and Dreams: *Vocabulary Quiz*

**Directions:** Match each vocabulary word with the correct meaning. Write the word on the line next to the meaning.

| anticipate | aspire | covet | enviable | inclination |
|---|---|---|---|---|
| desire | wistful | yearn | ambition | inspiration |
| mirage | cherish | ponder | intention | hankering |
| imagery | illusion | abstract | expectation | delusion |
| figment | visionary | whimsy | trance | |

1. _illusion_ appearance or feeling that misleads because it is not real
2. _anticipate_ look forward to; expect
3. _expectation_ anticipation; something expected
4. _enviable_ to be envied; worth having
5. _figment_ something imagined; made-up story
6. _cherish_ hold dear; treat with affection
7. _ponder_ consider carefully; think over
8. _aspire_ have an ambition for something
9. _delusion_ a false belief or opinion
10. _wistful_ longing; yearning
11. _abstract_ thought of apart from any particular object or real thing
12. _inclination_ preference; liking
13. _visionary_ person whose ideas seem impractical; dreamer
14. _intention_ purpose; design; plan
15. _whimsy_ an odd or fanciful notion
16. _desire_ a wanting or longing; strong wish
17. _trance_ state of unconsciousness somewhat like sleep
18. _ambition_ a strong desire for fame, honor, or wealth
19. _idealize_ think of or represent as perfect rather than as is actually true
20. _imagery_ pictures formed in the mind
21. _covet_ desire something that belongs to another
22. _yearn_ feel a longing or desire
23. _inspiration_ influence of thought and strong feelings on actions
24. _mirage_ an optical illusion, usually in the desert, at sea, or on a paved road
25. _hankering_ have a longing or craving

## Unit 11: Archaeology: Skills and Practice

**Directions:** For each word give a **synonym** from the vocabulary word list below. A **synonym** is a word that means the same or nearly the same.

| lithics | amber | mosaic | artifact | gemstone | expedition |
|---|---|---|---|---|---|
| archive | | | researcher | excavation | metamorphic |

1. jewel _gemstone_
2. tools _lithics_
3. journey _expedition_
4. resin _amber_
5. investigator _researcher_
6. changed _metamorphic_
7. dig _excavation_
8. objects _artifact_
9. record _archive_
10. design _mosaic_

**Did You Know?** The remains of Pompeii tell us about the past. When Mount Vesuvius erupted in 79 A.D., over 2000 people were unable to escape and were encased in lava. It happened so quickly that the people were killed in mid-action. The remains are being excavated to tell us about their everyday life untouched by time.

**Directions:** Write an **antonym** from the list of vocabulary words below on the line next to each word. An **antonym** is a word that means the opposite or nearly opposite.

tedious  relic  prehistoric  perseverance

1. yield _perseverance_
2. exciting _tedious_
3. new _prehistoric_  _relic_

**Directions:** Write a sentence for the following words on your own paper. Remember to check your spelling and punctuation.

archaeologist historian exhume paleontologist shards
anthropology architectural dating sedimentary igneous
ammonite

### Extend Your Vocabulary
1. Using plaster and shells, make your own fossil. Write down the steps it took to make one.
2. Make a list of dinosaurs; include both meat-eaters and plant-eaters.
3. Compare and contrast the architectural designs of different countries.
4. Tell about a time when you showed perseverance. Write about how you felt afterwards.

© Mark Twain Media, Inc., Publishers  43

## Unit 11: Archaeology: Vocabulary Quiz

**Directions:** Match each vocabulary word with the correct meaning. Write the word on the line next to the meaning.

| excavation | archaeologist | prehistoric | artifacts | lithics |
|---|---|---|---|---|
| anthropology | researcher | perseverance | archive | mosaic |
| expedition | architectural | sedimentary | shard | exhume |
| metamorphic | paleontologist | ammonite | amber | tedious |
| gemstone | igneous | historian | relic | dating |

1. _Sedimentary_ rock formed by the depositing of sediment
2. _archaeologist_ an expert in archaeology
3. _expedition_ journey for some special purpose
4. _artifacts_ anything made by human skill or work, espcially tools or weapons
5. _amber_ a hard, yellow or yellowish-brown gum; resin
6. _anthropology_ the science dealing with the origin, development, races, and customs of human beings
7. _architectural_ of the art of planning and designing buildings
8. _mosaic_ decorative design of small pieces of stone, glass, wood, etc. of different colors inlaid to form a design or picture
9. _metamorphic_ rock changed in structure by heat, moisture, and pressure
10. _exhume_ to dig out of the ground
11. _paleontologist_ an expert in the science of the forms of life existing in prehistoric time, such as fossil animals and plants
12. _dating_ to mark with characteristics typical of a particular period; to show the age of
13. _igneous_ rock formed by the cooling of melted rock material either within or on the surface of the earth
14. _prehistoric_ of or belonging to time before histories were written
15. _gemstone_ a precious or semi-precious stone, especially when cut and polished for ornamentation; jewel
16. _archive_ place where public records or historical documents are kept
17. _ammonite_ coiled, flat, chambered fossil shell of an extinct mollusk
18. _researcher_ person who does research; investigator
19. _relic_ thing left from the past
20. _perseverance_ sticking to a purpose or an aim
21. _tedious_ long and tiring
22. _excavation_ digging out; making hollow; hollowing out
23. _historian_ person who writes about history; expert in history
24. _shard_ broken pottery
25. _lithics_ stone tools

© Mark Twain Media, Inc., Publishers  44

## Unit 12: Clothing: Skills and Practice

**Directions:** For each word give a **synonym** from the vocabulary word list below. A **synonym** is a word that means the same or nearly the same.

breeches periwig babushka waders
bolero derby espadrille attire

1. water boots _waders_
2. clothing _attire_
3. bowler _derby_
4. scarf _babushka_
5. knickers _breeches_
6. sandal _espadrille_
7. wig _periwig_
8. jacket _bolero_

**Did You Know?** The Indian sari has no stiching, buttons, or zippers. It is a length of brightly-colored cloth that wraps around a woman's body. Even on a hot day, it is very cool and comfortable to wear.

**Directions:** Match the clothing to the correct country by placing the correct letter on the line.

_F_ 1. India A. kimono
_E_ 2. Ancient Greece B. sombrero
_D_ 3. Scotland C. panama
_B_ 4. Mexico D. tartan
_C_ 5. Central/South America E. tunic
_A_ 6. Japan F. sari and turban
_G_ 7. Latin America G. mantilla

**Directions:** Write a sentence for the following words on your own paper. Remember to check your spelling and punctuation.

clogs oxford kerchief frock wimple
jodhpurs coronet

### Extend Your Vocabulary
1. Make a list of clothing that you wear today that was popular a long time ago.
2. Research two or more of the vocabulary words that are clothing from another country.
3. Use some of the vocabulary words from this unit to begin your own list of different types of hats. Add more to the list.
4. Design your own piece of tartan cloth. Explain the reasons for the colors and design you picked.

© Mark Twain Media, Inc., Publishers  47

## Unit 12: Clothing: Vocabulary Quiz

**Directions:** Match each vocabulary word with the correct meaning. Write the word on the line next to the meaning.

| clog | derby | oxford | sombrero | babushka |
|---|---|---|---|---|
| sari | waders | periwig | espadrille | jodhpurs |
| tunic | bolero | panama | breeches | coronet |
| turban | bowler | tartan | crinoline | kerchief |
| wimple | frock | attire | mantilla | kimono |

1. _oxford_ kind of low shoe, laced over the instep
2. _tartan_ a plaid cloth
3. _periwig_ a wig in the seventeenth and eighteenth centuries
4. _attire_ clothing or dress
5. _sombrero_ a broad-brimmed hat worn in the southwestern United States, Mexico, and Spain
6. _frock_ a woman's or girl's dress; robe worn by a member of the clergy; a workman's outer shirt
7. _clog_ shoe with a thick, wooden sole
8. _kerchief_ piece of cloth worn over the head or around the neck
9. _bolero_ a short, loose jacket, with or without sleeves, that barely reaches to the waist
10. _sari_ a long piece of cotton or silk worn wound around the body with one end thrown over the head or shoulder
11. _derby_ a stiff hat with a rounded crown and narrow brim
12. _breeches_ short trousers fastened below the knees
13. _jodhpurs_ breeches for horseback riding, loose above the knees and close-fitting below the knees
14. _mantilla_ veil or scarf, often of lace, covering the hair and falling over the shoulders
15. _turban_ scarf wound around the head or around a cap, worn by men in parts of India and in some other countries
16. _kimono_ a loose outer garment held in place by a sash, worn by Japanese men and women
17. _babushka_ scarf worn on the head and tied under the chin
18. _tunic_ garment like a skirt or gown, worn by the ancient Greeks and Romans
19. _waders_ high, waterproof boots
20. _wimple_ cloth arranged in folds about the head, cheeks, chin, and neck
21. _bowler_ derby
22. _coronet_ a small crown indicating a rank of nobility below that of a king or queen
23. _crinoline_ a stiff cloth used as a lining to hold a skirt out or to make a coat collar stand up
24. _panama_ a fine hat woven from the young leaves of a palm-like plant of Central and South America
25. _espadrille_ a flat sandal, usually having a fabric upper and a flexible sole.

© Mark Twain Media, Inc., Publishers  48

## Panel 1 (top-left) — page 51

### Unit 13: Ancient Europe: *Skills and Practice*

**Directions:** For each word give a **synonym** from the vocabulary word list below. A **synonym** is a word that means the same or nearly the same.

| polis | forum | trireme | Christianity | helot |
|---|---|---|---|---|
| agora | tribune | absolute | revenge | gladiator |

1. religion _Christianity_    2. slave _helot_
3. city-state _polis_    4. official _tribune_
5. fighter _gladiator_    6. vessel _trireme_
7. whole _absolute_    8. vengeance _revenge_
9. marketplace _agora_ _forum_

**Did You Know?** Gladiators were usually criminals or slaves. Women were sometimes gladiators. They fought people and animals. The animals could even include elephants and giraffes.

**Directions:** Write an **antonym** from the list of vocabulary words below on the line next to each word. An **antonym** is a word that means the opposite or nearly opposite.

| shrewd | conquer | oppressive | civilization |
|---|---|---|---|

1. gentle _oppressive_    2. surrender _conquer_
3. ignorant _shrewd_    4. savagery _civilization_

**Directions:** Write a sentence for the following words on your own paper. Remember to check your spelling and punctuation.

| oligarchy | Spartans | philosophy | patrician | plebelan |
|---|---|---|---|---|
| aqueduct | empire | sculpture | period | legacy |

**Extend Your Vocabulary**

1. Make a Venn diagram comparing Rome to Greece.
2. Make a list of Greek or Roman traditions or beliefs that have been passed down to us. Include wedding traditions.
3. Research Julius Caesar. Write a report.
4. Illustrate a Roman soldier; include labels.

© Mark Twain Media, Inc., Publishers    51

## Panel 2 (top-right) — page 52

### Unit 13: Ancient Europe: *Vocabulary Quiz*

**Directions:** Match each vocabulary word with the correct meaning. Write the word on the line next to the meaning.

| philosophy | Helot | agora | oligarchy | Spartan |
|---|---|---|---|---|
| patrician | polis | forum | plebelan | tribune |
| gladiator | legacy | period | aqueduct | trireme |
| civilization | conquer | shrewd | oppressive | sculpture |
| Christianity | revenge | empire | absolute | soothsayer |

1. _conquer_ to defeat or subdue by force
2. _helot_ a person captured by Sparta and forced to live as a slave
3. _absolute_ free from any imperfection or lack; whole; entire; complete
4. _Spartan_ person who was born in or lived in Sparta
5. _trireme_ Greek sailing vessel
6. _plebeian_ a member of the common people in ancient Rome
7. _period_ portion of time
8. _aqueduct_ a large stone structure built by Romans to carry water from one place to another
9. _sculpture_ the art of making figures by carving, modeling, or casting
10. _agora_ the central marketplace in ancient Athens and the site of numerous temples and government buildings
11. _soothsayer_ person who claims to foretell the future; person who predicts
12. _philosophy_ the study of the nature and purpose of life; the search for the truth
13. _oppressive_ cruel or unjust
14. _polis_ a city-state in ancient Greece
15. _legacy_ something handed down from an ancestor or predecessor
16. _civilization_ a society that has achieved a high level of culture such as systems of government, religion, and learning
17. _revenge_ harm done in return for a wrong; vengeance
18. _forum_ a marketplace in the center of ancient Rome surrounded by public buildings
19. _empire_ a group of lands and people under one government
20. _oligarchy_ a government that is run by a few people, usually by members of rich and powerful families
21. _shrewd_ having a sharp mind; showing a keen wit; clever
22. _patrician_ a member of a class of wealthy families who held all the power in the early Roman Republic
23. _Christianity_ the religion based on the teachings of Christ as they appear in the Bible
24. _gladiator_ a person who fought in the Roman Colosseum to entertain the public
25. _tribune_ an elected official in ancient Rome who represented the interests of plebeians

© Mark Twain Media, Inc., Publishers    52

## Panel 3 (bottom-left) — page 55

### Unit 14: Medieval Times: *Skills and Practice*

**Directions:** For each word give a **synonym** from the vocabulary word list below. A **synonym** is a word that means the same or nearly the same.

| Influence | guild | lord | pilgrimage | crusades |
|---|---|---|---|---|
| minstrel | manor | flock | self-sufficient | artisan |

1. organization _guild_    2. noble _lord_
3. independent _self-sufficient_    4. journey _pilgrimage_
5. entertainer _minstrel_    6. craftsman _artisan_
7. crowd _flock_    8. estate _manor_
9. persuade _influence_    10. holy wars _crusade_

**Did You Know?** Each noble family had its own unique pattern on their coat of arms or shield. Each shield could have simple shapes such as stars and crosses; some had more elaborate designs such as ravens, castles, or swords. When the nobleman married, a new coat of arms was made, showing half from the man's shield and half from the woman's shield.

**Directions:** Write an **antonym** from the list of vocabulary words below on the line next to each word. An **antonym** is a word that means the opposite or nearly opposite.

| knight | apprentice | saint | monastery |
|---|---|---|---|

1. convent _monastery_    2. journeyman _apprentice_
3. sinner _saint_    4. page _knight_

**Directions:** Write a sentence for the following words on your own paper. Remember to check your spelling and punctuation.

| joust | feudalism | fief | vassal | Magna Carta |
|---|---|---|---|---|
| troubadour | serf | | | |

**Extend Your Vocabulary**

1. Research a famous person who lived during medieval times. Write a report.
2. Illustrate a shield that would represent your family.
3. What is jousting? Research it and write a mini report.
4. Make a list of famous nuns and monks who lived during the Middle Ages.

© Mark Twain Media, Inc., Publishers    55

## Panel 4 (bottom-right) — page 56

### Unit 14: Medieval Times: *Vocabulary Quiz*

**Directions:** Match each vocabulary word with the correct meaning. Write the word on the line next to the meaning.

| joust | feudalism | lord | fief | vassal |
|---|---|---|---|---|
| monastery | pilgrimage | serf | manor | knight |
| influence | apprentice | page | flock | convent |
| journeyman | Magna Carta | saint | squire | minstrel |
| self-sufficient | troubadour | crusade | guild | artisan |

1. _journeyman_ person in the Middle Ages who had completed his apprenticeship and was paid for his work
2. _lord_ a noble in the Middle Ages
3. _guild_ an organization of people who practiced the same craft, formed to set standards and promote the interests of the craft
4. _joust_ a combat with lances between two knights on horseback
5. _saint_ according to Roman Catholic teachings, a person believed to be especially holy
6. _fief_ large piece of land granted by the king to a lord in exchange for his loyalty
7. _minstrel_ singer or musician in the Middle Ages who entertained the household of a noble
8. _knight_ son of a noble who was a trained soldier and gave military service in exchange for the right to hold land
9. _apprentice_ person who lived and worked, without pay, with a master craftsman in order to learn a trade
10. _serf_ person who was bound to live and work on the land of a noble
11. _flock_ gather in a large group or crowd
12. _convent_ religious community in which nuns lead simple lives of work and prayer
13. _Magna Carta_ a document, drawn up by an English noble in 1215, that spelled out certain rights and limited the king's power
14. _feudalism_ an economic and political system of Europe in the Middle Ages based on certain obligations
15. _troubadour_ one of the lyric poets and composers of southern France, eastern Spain, and northern Italy from the 1000s to the 1200s
16. _vassal_ person during the Middle Ages who promised to fight for his lord when needed, in exchange for land
17. _artisan_ person skilled in some industry or trade; craftsman
18. _monastery_ a religious community in which monks lead simple lives of work and prayer
19. _squire_ young man who attended a knight until he became a knight
20. _manor_ self-sufficient farming estate where nobles and serfs lived and worked
21. _crusade_ a series of "holy wars" in which European Christians attempted to recapture the Holy Land
22. _pilgrimage_ journey to a holy place for a religious purpose
23. _self-sufficient_ asking no help; independent
24. _influence_ power of acting on others and having an effect without using force
25. _page_ a youth preparing to become a knight

© Mark Twain Media, Inc., Publishers    56

## Unit 15: Energy: *Skills and Practice*

Vocabulary Building: Grade 6
Unit 15: Energy: *Skills and Practice*
Name: _____ Date: _____

**Directions:** For each word give a **synonym** from the vocabulary word list below. A **synonym** is a word that means the same or nearly the same.

| reactor | energy | molecule | anthracite | pulley |
| matter | turbine | nuclear | deposit | circuit |

1. power _energy_
2. coal _anthracite_
3. engine _turbine_
4. lay down _deposit_
5. hookup _circuit_
6. machine _pulley_
7. atomic _nuclear_
8. substance _matter_
9. particle _molecule_
10. pile _reactor_

**Did You Know?** If you eat a small apple, it will give you enough energy to sleep for thirty minutes.

**Directions:** Match the vocabulary word to each of the related clues. Write the word on the line.

| radiation | hydroelectric | solar | resources | electromagnetic |

1. sun _solar_
2. wealth of country _resources_
3. water power _hydroelectric_
4. radio waves _electromagnetic_
5. radioactive _radiation_

**Directions:** Write a sentence for the following words on your own paper. Remember to check your spelling and punctuation.

| electricity | laser | friction | lever | nonrenewable |
| renewable | atom | | | |

### Extend Your Vocabulary

1. Make an energy cycle. Include sun, plants, animals, and so on.
2. Using the Internet, find an experiment on energy. With a partner, perform the experiment and share with the class what you have learned.
3. Research the conservation of energy. Write a report.
4. Make a list of natural resources.

59

## Unit 15: Energy: *Vocabulary Quiz*

Vocabulary Building: Grade 6
Unit 15: Energy: *Vocabulary Quiz*
Name: _____ Date: _____

**Directions:** Match each vocabulary word with the correct meaning. Write the word on the line next to the meaning.

| deposit | energy | hydroelectric | nuclear | atom |
| reactor | electron | electromagnetic | proton | solar |
| molecule | radiation | electricity | neutron | laser |
| anthracite | resources | nonrenewable | turbine | matter |
| renewable | friction | pulley | lever | circuit |

1. _resources_ actual and potential wealth of a country; natural resources
2. _hydroelectric_ developing electricity from water power
3. _electricity_ form of energy that can produce light, heat, motion, and magnetic force
4. _electron_ tiny particle carrying one unit of negative electricity
5. _laser_ device that produces a very narrow and intense beam of light with one wave length going in only one direction
6. _solar_ of the sun
7. _friction_ force between surfaces that resists the movement of one surface past the other surface
8. _deposit_ put down; lay down
9. _anthracite_ coal that burns with very little smoke and flame; hard coal
10. _reactor_ vat or apparatus for the release of atomic energy by a controlled chain reaction; nuclear pile
11. _renewable_ able to be made new again; get again; fill again
12. _radiation_ particles or electromagnetic waves given off by the atoms and molecules of a radioactive substance as a result of nuclear decay
13. _turbine_ engine or motor consisting of a wheel with vanes that is made to revolve by the force of water, steam, or air
14. _energy_ ability to do work; make things happen
15. _lever_ bar that turns on a fixed support called the fulcrum and is used to transmit effort and motion
16. _neutron_ an atomic particle that is neutral electrically and has about the same mass as a proton
17. _matter_ any physical thing; solid; liquid, or gas that takes up space
18. _atom_ the smallest particle of an element that retains the characteristics of that element
19. _nonrenewable_ not able to make again; cannot be replaced or fixed
20. _molecule_ the smallest particle into which an element or compound can be divided without changing its chemical or physical properties
21. _circuit_ arrangement of wiring and tubes, for example, forming electrical connections; hookup
22. _proton_ a tiny particle in the nucleus of the atom, carrying one unit of positive electricity
23. _pulley_ a simple machine made up of at least one grooved wheel and a rope, chain, or belt
24. _electromagnetic_ of or caused by an electromagnet
25. _nuclear_ of nuclei or a nucleus, especially the nucleus of an atom

60

## Unit 16: Lengthy Words: *Skills and Practice*

Vocabulary Building: Grade 6
Unit 16: Lengthy Words: *Skills and Practice*
Name: _____ Date: _____

**Directions:** For each word give a **synonym** from the vocabulary word list below. A **synonym** is a word that means the same or nearly the same.

| fraudulent | venomous | spontaneous | vacuous |
| facsimile | ultimate | pandemonium | quandary |
| mesmerize | recurrence | predicament | insinuate |
| bamboozle | serpentine | obstinate | |

1. repetition _recurrence_
2. poisonous _venomous_
3. copy _facsimile_
4. hypnotize _mesmerize_
5. trick _bamboozle_
6. hint _insinuate_
7. dishonest _fraudulent_
8. stupid _vacuous_
9. confusion _pandemonium_
10. final _ultimate_
11. twisting _serpentine_
12. stubborn _obstinate_
13. dilemma _quandary_
_predicament_
14. impulsive _spontaneous_

**Did You Know?** Some people read right to left and back to front. To read a book in Arabic or Hebrew, it is necessary to start on the last page reading right to left and continue to the front.

**Directions:** Write a sentence for each of the following words on your own paper. Remember to check your spelling and punctuation.

| cadence | enunciate | interlace | lethargy | menagerie |
| metropolis | phenomenon | euphoria | kleptomania | virtuoso |

### Extend Your Vocabulary

1. Make a class list of lengthy words. Look for root words that may be present.
2. Practice with a partner enunciating a list of lengthy words.
3. Research a natural phenomenon such as "Old Faithful."
4. Write about a time when you were in a predicament. What happened? How did you feel? How did it turn out?

63

## Unit 16: Lengthy Words: *Vocabulary Quiz*

Vocabulary Building: Grade 6
Unit 16: Lengthy Words: *Vocabulary Quiz*
Name: _____ Date: _____

**Directions:** Match each vocabulary word with the correct meaning. Write the word on the line next to the meaning.

| bamboozle | cadence | enunciate | facsimile | fraudulent |
| lethargy | menagerie | mesmerize | metropolis | pandemonium |
| predicament | quandary | spontaneous | vacuous | venomous |
| euphoria | insinuate | kleptomania | obstinate | recurrence |
| serpentine | ultimate | virtuoso | interlace | phenomenon |

1. _insinuate_ suggest in an indirect way; hint
2. _bamboozle_ impose upon; cheat; trick
3. _serpentine_ winding; twisting
4. _mesmerize_ hypnotize
5. _venomous_ poisonous
6. _interlace_ to unite by passing over; weave together.
7. _vacuous_ showing no intelligence; senseless
8. _metropolis_ large city; important center
9. _ultimate_ coming at the end; last; final
10. _quandary_ state of perplexity or uncertainty
11. _kleptomania_ abnormal, irresistible desire to steal
12. _cadence_ the measure or beat of music, dancing, or any movement regularly repeating itself
13. _euphoria_ feeling of happiness and bodily well-being
14. _facsimile_ an exact copy or likeness
15. _recurrence_ occur again; repetition
16. _menagerie_ collection of wild animals kept in cages for exhibition
17. _virtuoso_ person skilled in the techniques of an art, especially in playing a musical instrument
18. _predicament_ an unpleasant, difficult, or bad situation
19. _obstinate_ not giving in; stubborn
20. _fraudulent_ cheating; dishonest
21. _enunciate_ speak or pronounce words
22. _pandemonium_ wild uproar or confusion
23. _lethargy_ drowsy dullness; lack of energy
24. _spontaneous_ caused by natural impulse or desire; not planned beforehand
25. _phenomenon_ fact, event, or circumstance that can be observed

64

## Unit 17: Travel: *Skills and Practice*

Vocabulary Building: Grade 6 — Unit 17: Travel: *Skills and Practice*

Name: _____ Date: _____

**Directions:** For each word give a **synonym** from the vocabulary word list below. A **synonym** is a word that means the same or nearly the same.

| brochure | tourist | souvenir | shilling | jaunt | reminiscence |
| caravan | chronicle | shilling | exotic | accommodations |
| cargo | garb |

1. lodging __accommodations__
3. clothes __garb__
5. history __chronicle__
7. goods __cargo__
9. keepsake __souvenir__
11. pamphlet __brochure__
2. strange __exotic__
4. money __shilling__
6. excursion __jaunt__
8. recollection __reminiscence__
10. traveling group __caravan__
12. vacationer __tourist__

**Did You Know?** The world's longest car has 26 wheels. It actually has room for a tiny swimming pool.

**Directions:** Write an **antonym** from the list of vocabulary words below on the line next to each word. An **antonym** is a word that means the opposite or nearly opposite.

| landlubber | destination | unscheduled | trek |

1. sailor __landlubber__
2. planned __unscheduled__
3. sprint __trek__
4. origin __destination__

**Directions:** Write a sentence for the following words on your own paper. Remember to check your spelling and punctuation.

| bon voyage | itinerary | Hovercraft | jet lag | getaway |
| travelog | airfare | excursion |

**Extend Your Vocabulary**

1. Make a travel brochure for an exotic getaway.
2. Make a list of at least ten national hotel chains.
3. Reminisce with a grandparent or great aunt or uncle about their childhood. Use a Venn diagram to compare their childhood to yours.
4. Describe a favorite souvenir. Where did it come from? Who bought it? What meaning does it have for you?

© Mark Twain Media, Inc., Publishers — 67

## Unit 17: Travel: *Vocabulary Quiz*

**Directions:** Match each vocabulary word with the correct meaning. Write the word on the line next to the meaning.

| excursion | bon voyage | trek | itinerary | reminiscence |
| souvenir | caravan | cargo | destination | accommodations |
| shilling | chronicle | garb | airfare | unscheduled |
| exotic | travelog | jaunt | Hovercraft | brochure |
| jet lag | tourist | outing | getaway | landlubber |

1. __excursion__ a short trip taken for interest or pleasure, often by a number of people together
2. __jaunt__ a short journey or excursion, especially for pleasure
3. __caravan__ a group of merchants or pilgrims, traveling together for safety through difficult or dangerous country
4. __Hovercraft__ trademark for a vehicle that travels a few feet above the surface of land or water on a cushion of air
5. __exotic__ foreign; strange; not native
6. __shilling__ a former unit of money in Great Britain equal to 12 pence or 1/20 of a pound
7. __bon voyage__ French phrase meaning pleasant journey
8. __chronicle__ record of events in the order in which they took place; history; story
9. __souvenir__ something given or kept for remembrance; a keepsake
10. __getaway__ a short period of rest and relaxation
11. __outing__ a short pleasure trip, walk, or airing
12. __unscheduled__ not planned
13. __trek__ travel slowly by any means
14. __airfare__ the money that a person pays to ride in an airplane
15. __garb__ the way one is dressed
16. __tourist__ person traveling for pleasure
17. __itinerary__ route of travel; plan of travel; record of travel; guidebook for travelers
18. __brochure__ pamphlet
19. __landlubber__ person not used to being on ships; person who is awkward on board a ship due to lack of experience
20. __jet lag__ the delayed effects, such as tiredness, felt by a person after a long flight in a jet plane through several time zones
21. __cargo__ load of goods carried by a ship or plane
22. __travelog__ lecture describing travel, usually accompanied by pictures or films
23. __destination__ place to which a person or thing is going or is being sent
24. __accommodations__ lodging and sometimes food as well
25. __reminiscence__ a remembering; recalling past persons or events; recollection

© Mark Twain Media, Inc., Publishers — 68

## Unit 18: Positive and Negative: *Skills and Practice*

**Directions:** For each word give a **synonym** from the vocabulary word list below. A **synonym** is a word that means the same or nearly the same.

| parry | betterment | gratuity | unsurpassed | extinction |
| revoke | negligence | infallible | affirmation | disclaimer |
| deter |

1. improvement __betterment__
3. tip __gratuity__
5. evade __parry__
7. hinder __deter__
9. assertion __affirmation__
11. destruction __extinction__
2. neglect __negligence__
4. withdraw __revoke__
6. sure __infallible__
8. superior __unsurpassed__
10. denial __disclaimer__

**Did You Know?** In southern Africa children squat or sit when speaking to adults, out of respect for them.

**Directions:** Write an **antonym** from the list of vocabulary words below on the line next to each word. An **antonym** is a word that means the opposite or nearly opposite.

| positive | certainty | refusal | contradiction | rejection | assurance |

1. agreement __contradiction__
3. acceptance __refusal__
4. doubt __certainty__
2. negative __positive__
__rejection__
__assurance__

**Directions:** Write a sentence for the following words on your own paper. Remember to check your spelling and punctuation.

| invalidate | prohibition | retraction | resistant | repulsive |
| extinguish | decisive | denial |

**Extend Your Vocabulary**

1. Write a short report on an animal or plant facing extinction.
2. Make a list of positive gestures.
3. Write about a time when someone was being negative and how it affected you.
4. Write a list of suggestions for the betterment of your classroom.

© Mark Twain Media, Inc., Publishers — 71

## Unit 18: Positive and Negative: *Vocabulary Quiz*

**Directions:** Match each vocabulary word with the correct meaning. Write the word on the line next to the meaning.

| denial | negativity | negligence | retraction | contradiction |
| revoke | rejection | affirmation | disclaimer | prohibition |
| refusal | resistant | repulsive | certainty | unsurpassed |
| deter | assurance | extinction | extinguish | invalidate |
| parry | gratuity | betterment | infallible | decisive |

1. __decisive__ conclusive; critically important; showing determination or firmness
2. __denial__ a saying that something is not true
3. __extinction__ bringing to an end; wiping out; destruction
4. __retraction__ a taking back; withdrawal of a promise
5. __assurance__ statement intended to make a person more sure or certain
6. __affirmation__ positive statement; assertion
7. __parry__ ward off; turn aside; evade
8. __revoke__ take back; repeal; cancel; withdraw
9. __extinguish__ put out; bring to an end; wipe out; destroy
10. __repulsive__ causing strong dislike or aversion
11. __deter__ keep back; discourage or hinder
12. __contradiction__ denial; statement or act that contradicts another
13. __betterment__ a making better; improvement
14. __negativity__ negative quality or condition
15. __invalidate__ make valueless; cause to be worthless
16. __rejection__ a rejecting; refusing to take
17. __infallible__ free from error; not able to be mistaken; sure
18. __prohibition__ act of forbidding by law or authority; act of preventing
19. __gratuity__ present of money in return for service; tip
20. __resistant__ resisting; opposing
21. __unsurpassed__ not capable of being improved upon; superior
22. __certainty__ freedom from doubt
23. __refusal__ act of refusing
24. __negligence__ lack of proper care or attention; neglect
25. __disclaimer__ denial; a disclaiming

© Mark Twain Media, Inc., Publishers — 72

## Unit 19: Newspaper: Skills and Practice

**Directions:** Categorize each of the vocabulary words below and write the word on the line under the correct category.

masthead  editorial  filler  stringer  teaser
feature  wire editor  logo  source  subhead
follow-up  deskman

**Parts of the newspaper**
teaser
masthead
subhead
feature
filler
follow-up
editorial
logo

**People dealing with the newspaper**
source
wire editor
deskman
stringer

**Did You Know?** America's first published newspaper was issued on April 24, 1704. John Campbell was the first editor.

**Directions:** Write a sentence for the following words on your own paper. Remember to check your spelling and punctuation.

backgrounder  byline  copyright  dummy  libel
circulation  typo  deadline  proof  morgue
wirephoto  newsprint  spot news

**Extend Your Vocabulary**

1. Make a class newspaper. Divide the articles and add weather, sports, comics, and so on.
2. Interview a newspaper reporter. Write about it.
3. Make a list of titles of popular newspapers.
4. Edit a partner's writing piece for errors. Use proofreading marks to make corrections.

## Unit 19: Newspaper: Vocabulary Quiz

**Directions:** Match each vocabulary word with the correct meaning. Write the word on the line next to the meaning.

byline  copyright  typo  subhead  editorial
morgue  stringer  logo  dummy  Wirephoto
teaser  circulation  proof  source  deskman
spot news  masthead  filler  feature  backgrounder
deadline  wire editor  libel  follow-up  newsprint

1. byline the name of the writer printed at the head of a story
2. filler written material of minor importance used to fill extra space in the news columns
3. dummy diagram of a newspaper page that shows the placement of headlines, stories, pictures, etc.
4. Wirephoto Associated Press service that transmits pictures to subscribing newspapers
5. morgue an old term for the newspaper's library where files of clippings, photos, and microfilm of past issues and other materials are contained
6. Circulation total number of copies of the newspaper distributed to subscribers and news vendors in a single day
7. teaser an announcement placed prominently in the newspaper, often on page one, telling about an interesting story elsewhere in the paper
8. masthead formal statement of a paper's name, officers, point of publication, and other information
9. Copyright legal protection to an author from unauthorized use of his work
10. feature a special story or article in a newspaper, often prominently displayed
11. typo short for "typographical error"
12. backgrounder a story that summarizes the background of a current matter in the news
13. editorial an expression of opinion of the newspaper's editors
14. deskman copy editor
15. logo short for "logotype"
16. follow-up story which adds more information to a story already printed
17. spot news news obtained firsthand; fresh news
18. deadline the time a story must be ready to print
19. libel false communication that injures the reputation of an individual
20. wire editor edits news supplied by the news agencies or "wire services"
21. Stringer part-time writer, usually covering a particular area or subject, often paid according to the amount of his or her copy printed in the paper
22. newsprint a grade of paper made of wood pulp, used for printing newspapers
23. source supplier of information, such as a person, book, or survey
24. proof an impression of a printed page or story
25. subhead a one- or two-line heading used to divide sections of a story

## Unit 20: Amounts: Skills and Practice

**Directions:** For each word give a **synonym** from the vocabulary word list below. A **synonym** is a word that means the same or nearly the same.

meager  amplitude  humongous  multitude  median
trifle  diminutive  approximation  extensive  surpass
mean

1. monstrosity humongous
2. sparse meager
3. excel surpass
4. far-reaching extensive
5. tinge trifle
6. abundance amplitude
7. estimate approximation
8. middle median
9. average mean
10. minute diminutive
11. crowd multitude

**Did You Know?** When averaging numbers, the minimum is the smallest value and the maximum is the largest value. Cherrapunji, India, is one of the world's wettest places, receiving a maximum average of nearly 430 inches of rain per year.

**Directions:** Write an antonym from the list of vocabulary words below on the line next to each word. An antonym is a word that means the opposite or nearly opposite.

infinite  adequate  scant  accumulate

1. insufficient adequate
2. disperse accumulate
3. limited infinite
4. plentiful scant

**Directions:** Write a sentence for the following words on your own paper. Remember to check your spelling and punctuation.

batch  voluminous  caliber  scruple  monstrosity
mode  gigantean  sparse  tinge

**Extend Your Vocabulary**

1. Read the book How Much is a Million. Write a reaction.
2. Make two lists of words, one meaning "large" and one meaning "small."
3. Find a Guinness Book of World Records and record some very large or very small records.
4. Read some fairy tales that have gigantean characters. List them.

## Unit 20: Amounts: Vocabulary Quiz

**Directions:** Match each vocabulary word with the correct meaning. Write the word on the line next to the meaning.

meager  accumulate  mean  extensive  approximation
sparse  amplitude  infinite  multitude  monstrosity
trifle  humongous  scant  caliber  voluminous
batch  gigantean  median  surpass  diminutive
mode  scruple  tinge  quantum  adequate

1. median in the middle
2. adequate as much as is needed for a particular purpose; sufficient; enough
3. voluminous of great size; large; very bulky
4. sparse scanty; meager
5. humongous extremely large; enormous
6. accumulate collect little by little; pile up; gather
7. scruple apothecary's measure of weight equal to 20 grains
8. caliber amount of ability
9. mean halfway between two extremes; average
10. extensive of great extent; far-reaching; large
11. tinge a very small amount; trace
12. quantum the basic unit of radiant energy; the smallest amount of energy capable of existing independently
13. gigantean like a giant; mighty; gigantic
14. monstrosity huge; enormous
15. scant barely enough; barely full; bare
16. batch quantity of anything made as one lot or set; number of persons or things taken together
17. mode the value or values that occur most often in a set of data
18. surpass do better than; be greater than; excel
19. diminutive very small; tiny; minute
20. multitude a great many; crowd
21. trifle a small amount; little bit
22. infinite without limits or bounds; endless
23. meager poor or scanty
24. amplitude quantity that is more than enough; abundance
25. approximation a nearly correct amount; estimate

---

## Unit 21: Peace and War: *Skills and Practice*

**Directions:** For each word give a **synonym** from the vocabulary word list below. A **synonym** is a word that means the same or nearly the same.

| bellicose | humanity | chaos | disturbance | justice |
| injustice | tyrannical | tactic | serenity | harmony |
| arbitration | tranquillity | | | |

1. cruel *tyrannical*
2. mankind *humanity*
3. maneuver *tactic*
4. combative *bellicose*
5. agreement *harmony*
6. partiality *injustice*
7. fairness *justice*
8. settlement *arbitration*
9. disorder *disturbance*  *chaos*
10. calmness *serenity*  *tranquillity*

> **Did You Know?** The Maori people of New Zealand stick out their tongues to say "hello." They welcome guests by staring at them fiercely and sticking out their tongues.

**Directions:** Write an **antonym** from the list of vocabulary words below on the line next to each word. An **antonym** is a word that means the opposite or nearly opposite.

| animosity | intolerance | placid | discord | amicable |

1. agreement *discord*
2. love *animosity*
3. noisy *placid*
4. warlike *amicable*
5. cooperative *intolerance*

**Directions:** Write a sentence for the following words on your own paper. Remember to check your spelling and punctuation.

| amity | antagonism | quarrel | tolerance | strife |
| truce | cooperative | combative | | |

**Extend Your Vocabulary**

1. Make a list of symbols of peace. Illustrate some of them, for example: peace sign, handshake.
2. Research the Peace Corps and what it stands for. Write a report.
3. Discuss the meaning of the figurative phrase, "to hold one's peace."
4. List the reasons for World War I and World War II.

---

## Unit 21: Peace and War: *Vocabulary Quiz*

**Directions:** Match each vocabulary word with the correct meaning. Write the word on the line next to the meaning.

| cooperative | intolerance | chaos | serenity | tranquillity |
| animosity | amicable | truce | discord | disturbance |
| antagonism | humanity | strife | justice | tolerance |
| injustice | combative | amity | tactic | bellicose |
| tyrannical | arbitration | placid | quarrel | harmony |

1. *humanity* human beings; people; mankind
2. *disturbance* a disturbing or a being disturbed; disorder; confusion
3. *strife* a quarreling; fighting
4. *chaos* very great confusion; complete disorder
5. *injustice* being unjust; lack of justice
6. *antagonism* active opposition; hostility
7. *tolerance* a willingness to be tolerant; a putting up with people whose opinions or ways differ from one's own
8. *tranquillity* calmness; peacefulness; quiet
9. *placid* pleasantly calm or peaceful; quiet
10. *serenity* peace and quiet; calmness
11. *tyrannical* of or like a tyrant; cruel; unjust
12. *truce* a stop in fighting; temporary peace
13. *amity* peace and friendship
14. *cooperative* wanting or willing to work together with others
15. *bellicose* fond of fighting; warlike
16. *amicable* having or showing a friendly attitude; peaceable
17. *arbitration* settlement of a dispute by the decision of a judge, umpire, or committee
18. *discord* a difference of opinion; disagreement; disputing
19. *tactic* maneuver
20. *quarrel* an angry dispute; a fight with words
21. *combative* ready to fight; fond of fighting
22. *intolerance* unwillingness to let others do and think as they choose
23. *justice* just conduct; fair dealing; fairness
24. *animosity* violent hatred; active dislike
25. *harmony* agreement of feeling, ideas, or actions; getting on well together

---

## Unit 22: Health: *Skills and Practice*

**Directions:** For each word give a **synonym** from the vocabulary word list below. A **synonym** is a word that means the same or nearly the same.

| coronary | contagious | respiration | convalescence | epidemic |
| laceration | sterilization | immunity | contaminated | vigor |
| diagnosis | vaccination | | | |

1. catching *contagious*
2. recovery *convalescence*
3. tear *laceration*
4. resistance *immunity*
5. inoculation *vaccination*
6. breathing *respiration*
7. heart *coronary*
8. strength *vigor*
9. germ-free *sterilization*
10. polluted *contaminated*
11. analysis *diagnosis*
12. infestation *epidemic*

> **Did You Know?** Earl Dickerson invented the Band-Aid. He put small squares of cloth onto pieces of tape, covering them completely to stop the glue from drying out.

**Directions:** Read the following list of words and circle those that are parts of the human body.

synapse   gene   hygiene   neuron   heredity   pituitary   life span

**Directions:** Write a sentence for the following words on your own paper. Remember to check your spelling and punctuation.

| paralysis | tetanus | chemotherapy | heredity | gene |
| lifespan | synapse | contaminated | hygiene | neuron |
| pituitary | antibiotic | metabolism | quarantine | |

**Extend Your Vocabulary**

1. Make a list of contagious ailments.
2. Invite a doctor or nurse to your school. Have a question and answer session.
3. Research vaccinations and why children need them.
4. As a class, visit a younger classroom and explain good hygiene.

---

## Unit 22: Health: *Vocabulary Quiz*

**Directions:** Match each vocabulary word with the correct meaning. Write the word on the line next to the meaning.

| contagious | paralysis | convalescence | coronary | gene |
| tetanus | laceration | chemotherapy | heredity | vigor |
| immunity | metabolism | contaminated | life span | neuron |
| synapse | pituitary | quarantine | hygiene | epidemic |
| antibiotic | respiration | sterilization | vaccination | diagnosis |

1. *neuron* one of the cells of which the brain, spinal cord, and nerves are composed; nerve cell
2. *convalescence* the gradual recovery of health and strength after an illness
3. *sterilization* free from living germs
4. *chemotherapy* the use of chemical agents in the treatment or control of disease
5. *vigor* active strength or force
6. *immunity* resistance to disease or poison
7. *respiration* act of inhaling and exhaling; breathing
8. *contagious* spreading by contact; catching
9. *quarantine* keep away from others for a time to prevent the spread of an infectious disease
10. *coronary* of or having to do with either of the two arteries that supply blood to the muscular tissue of the heart
11. *pituitary* a small, oval endocrine gland situated at the base of the brain
12. *gene* a minute part of a chromosome that influences the inheritance and development of some characteristic
13. *contaminated* made impure by contact; defiled; polluted
14. *metabolism* process by which all living things turn food into energy and living tissue
15. *synapse* place where a nerve impulse passes from one nerve cell to another
16. *paralysis* a lessening or loss of the power of motion or sensation in any part of the body
17. *vaccination* inoculate with a vaccine
18. *laceration* a rough tear; mangled place
19. *epidemic* the rapid spread of disease so that many people have it at the same time
20. *heredity* the passing on of physical or mental characteristics from parent to offspring by means of genes
21. *antibiotic* substance produced by a living organism, especially a bacterium or fungus, that destroys or weakens germs
22. *life span* the period between birth and death during which a living thing is functional
23. *hygiene* rules of health; science of keeping well
24. *tetanus* disease caused by certain bacteria, usually entering the body through wounds, characterized by violent spasms and stiffness of many muscles
25. *diagnosis* act or process of determining the type of illness or disease of a person or animal by examination and careful study of the symptoms

---

## Unit 23: Movement: *Skills and Practice*

Vocabulary Building: Grade 6 — Unit 23: Movement: *Skills and Practice*

Name: _____ Date: _____

**Directions:** For each word give a **synonym** from the vocabulary word list below. A **synonym** is a word that means the same or nearly the same.

| canter | roving | tread | mingle | scurry |
|--------|--------|-------|--------|--------|
| fidgety | flurry | brisk | fleet | |

1. scuttle — scurry
2. gust — flurry
3. roaming — roving
4. restless — fidgety
5. gallop — canter
6. rapid — fleet
7. walk — tread
8. lively — brisk
9. mix — mingle

**Did You Know?** If you stayed in bed all day, you would still travel about 1.5 million miles. That is how far the earth moves through space in 24 hours as it goes around the sun.

**Directions:** Write an **antonym** from the list of vocabulary words below on the line next to each word. An **antonym** is a word that means the opposite or nearly opposite.

| mobility | acceleration | nimble | recede | linger |
|----------|--------------|--------|--------|--------|
| fluctuate | perpetual | | | |

1. deceleration — acceleration
2. hasten — linger
3. propel — recede
4. remain — fluctuate
5. immobility — mobility
6. temporary — perpetual
7. awkward — nimble

**Directions:** Write a sentence for the following words on your own paper. Remember to check your spelling and punctuation.

| totter | transverse | gait | hover | deviate |
|--------|-----------|------|-------|---------|
| straggle | kinesthetic | propel | scuttle | |

### Extend Your Vocabulary

1. Categorize this unit's words under certain headings, such as slow and fast movements.
2. Match as many of the movements as you can with a particular animal, such as hover - hummingbird; scurry - mouse, and so on.
3. Research the different muscles and how they allow our body to move. Write a report.
4. Make a list of oxymorons such as these: restless sleep, gentle turbulence, slow jet.

© Mark Twain Media, Inc., Publishers — 91

---

## Unit 23: Movement: *Vocabulary Quiz*

Vocabulary Building: Grade 6 — Unit 23: Movement: *Vocabulary Quiz*

Name: _____ Date: _____

**Directions:** Match each vocabulary word with the correct meaning. Write the word on the line next to the meaning.

| brisk | perpetual | fluctuate | fleet | linger |
|-------|-----------|-----------|-------|--------|
| nimble | transverse | mobility | tread | flurry |
| scurry | kinesthetic | deviate | hover | canter |
| roving | acceleration | propel | recede | scuttle |
| totter | straggle | fidgety | mingle | gait |

1. deviate — turn aside from a way, course, truth, and so on.
2. fleet — swiftly moving; rapid
3. kinesthetic — having to do with sensations of motion from the muscles and joints
4. perpetual — never ceasing; continuous
5. acceleration — a speeding up or hastening
6. transverse — lying across; placed crosswise; crossing from side to side
7. fidgety — restless; uneasy
8. linger — stay on; go slowly
9. propel — drive forward; force ahead
10. brisk — quick and active; lively
11. straggle — wander in a scattered fashion
12. fluctuate — rise and fall; change continually; waver
13. scuttle — scamper; scurry
14. hover — stay in or near one place in the air
15. roving — wandering about; roaming; rambling
16. totter — walk with shaky, unsteady steps
17. flurry — a sudden gust
18. nimble — active and sure-footed; quick; agile
19. canter — gallop gently
20. mingle — to combine in a mixture; mix; blend
21. mobility — ability or readiness to move or be moved
22. scurry — run quickly; scamper; hurry
23. gait — the kind of steps used in going along; manner of walking or running
24. recede — go backward; move backward
25. tread — set the foot down; walk; step

© Mark Twain Media, Inc., Publishers — 92

---

## Unit 24: Law: *Skills and Practice*

Vocabulary Building: Grade 6 — Unit 24: Law: *Skills and Practice*

Name: _____ Date: _____

**Directions:** For each word give a **synonym** from the vocabulary word list below. A **synonym** is a word that means the same or nearly the same.

| witness | allegation | evidence | attest | law-abiding |
|---------|-----------|----------|--------|-------------|
| legality | penitentiary | culprit | larceny | testimony |

1. facts — evidence
2. lawfulness — legality
3. spectator — witness
4. theft — larceny
5. offender — culprit
6. testify — attest
7. proof — testimony
8. assertion — allegation
9. orderly — law-abiding
10. prison — penitentiary

**Did You Know?** The Babylonians were the first group of people to write down their own laws.

**Directions:** Write an **antonym** from the list of vocabulary words below on the line next to each word. An **antonym** is a word that means the opposite or nearly opposite.

| bungling | objection | legitimate | conviction | defendant | opponent |
|----------|-----------|------------|------------|-----------|----------|

1. friend — opponent
2. approval — objection
3. acquittal — conviction
4. unlawful — legitimate
5. competent — bungling
6. plaintiff — defendant

**Directions:** Write a sentence for the following words on your own paper. Remember to check your spelling and punctuation.

| disposition | verdict | subpoena | lawsuit | sequester |
|-------------|---------|----------|---------|-----------|
| accomplice | bylaw | summation | habeas corpus | |

### Extend Your Vocabulary

1. Make a list of famous lawyers.
2. Write the dialogue for a court scene; you make up the crime.
3. Make a list of classroom rules or laws.
4. Interview a lawyer. Publish it in a classroom newspaper.

© Mark Twain Media, Inc., Publishers — 95

---

## Unit 24: Law: *Vocabulary Quiz*

Vocabulary Building: Grade 6 — Unit 24: Law: *Vocabulary Quiz*

Name: _____ Date: _____

**Directions:** Match each vocabulary word with the correct meaning. Write the word on the line next to the meaning.

| bylaw | evidence | penitentiary | larceny | testimony |
|-------|----------|--------------|---------|-----------|
| verdict | witness | objection | opponent | conviction |
| bungling | allegation | subpoena | sequester | law-abiding |
| attest | lawsuit | accomplice | disposition | habeas corpus |
| culprit | defendant | legality | summation | legitimate |

1. legitimate — allowed or admitted by law; rightful; lawful
2. testimony — statement used for evidence
3. accomplice — person who knowingly aids another in committing a crime
4. defendant — person accused in a court of law
5. habeas corpus — order requiring that a prisoner be brought before a judge or into court to decide whether he or she is being held lawfully
6. conviction — act of proving or declaring guilty
7. law-abiding — obeying the law; peaceful and orderly
8. larceny — the unlawful taking and using of the personal property of another person; theft
9. sequester — remove or withdraw from public view
10. subpoena — an official written order commanding a person to appear in a court of law
11. summation — the final presentation of facts and arguments by the counsel for each side
12. opponent — person who is on the other side in a fight, game, or discussion
13. legality — accordance with the law; lawfulness
14. penitentiary — a prison for criminals
15. lawsuit — case in a court of law started by one person to claim something from another
16. evidence — anything that shows what is true and what is not; facts; proof
17. disposition — a disposing; settlement
18. verdict — the decision of a jury
19. culprit — person guilty of a fault or crime; offender
20. objection — something said in objecting; reason or argument against something
21. bungling — do or make in a clumsy, unskilled way
22. allegation — an accusation made without proof
23. witness — person who saw something happen; spectator; eyewitness
24. attest — give proof of; certify; bear witness; testify
25. bylaw — law made by a city, company, club, and so forth for the control of its own affairs

© Mark Twain Media, Inc., Publishers — 96

## Left worksheet

Name: _____   Date: _____

### Unit 25: Sports: *Skills and Practice*

**Directions:** For each word give a **synonym** from the vocabulary word list below. A **synonym** is a word that means the same or nearly the same.

| champion | modern | qualifying | stamina | elite |
| Olympian | amateur | popular | comrade | laurel |
| marathon | javelin | challenge | preliminary | luge |

1. sled _luge_
2. race _marathon_
3. spear _javelin_
4. leaves _laurel_
5. best _elite_
6. endurance _stamina_
7. preparatory _preliminary_
8. favorite _popular_
9. training _qualifying_
10. participant _Olympian_
11. friend _comrade_
12. present _modern_
13. contend _challenge_
14. novice _amateur_
15. winner _champion_

**Did You Know?** The first ancient Olympic Games were established in 776 B.C. They were held every four years in Olympia. Problems arose such as paying athletes and bribing judges. These problems brought an end to the ancient Olympic Games. They were not held again for 1500 years.

**Directions:** Write a sentence for the following words on your own paper. Remember to check your spelling and punctuation.

| international | protocol | biathlon | endurance | hurdles |
| commemorative | triathlon | sprints | equestrian | archery |

#### Extend Your Vocabulary

1. Compare and contrast the ancient Olympic Games to the modern Olympic Games.
2. Write a narrative piece about you participating in the Olympic Games. How would you feel? Which sport would you choose?
3. Research the Olympic symbol of the five rings. Write about it.
4. Make a list of sports in the summer and winter Olympic games.

© Mark Twain Media, Inc., Publishers          99

## Right worksheet

Name: _____   Date: _____

### Unit 25: Sports: *Vocabulary Quiz*

**Directions:** Match each vocabulary word with the correct meaning. Write the word on the line next to the meaning.

| international | laurel | marathon | javelin | champion |
| commemorative | elite | modern | protocol | biathlon |
| preliminary | luge | triathlon | archery | amateur |
| endurance | sprints | stamina | hurdles | comrade |
| challenge | Olympian | popular | equestrian | qualifying |

1. _archery_ practice or sport of shooting with a bow and arrow
2. _laurel_ the smooth, shining leaves of a small evergreen tree
3. _champion_ person who wins first place in a game or contest
4. _comrade_ a close companion and friend
5. _elite_ the choice or distinguished part; those thought of as the best people
6. _amateur_ person who does something for pleasure, not for money or as a profession
7. _javelin_ a lightweight spear thrown by hand
8. _preliminary_ coming before the main business; something preparatory
9. _equestrian_ having to do with horseback riding, horses, or horseback riders
10. _endurance_ power to last and to withstand hard wear
11. _modern_ present times
12. _stamina_ strength; endurance
13. _marathon_ a foot race of 26 miles, 385 yards
14. _popular_ liked by most people
15. _protocol_ rules of etiquette
16. _sprints_ race or any short spell of running, rowing, and so forth at maximum speed
17. _luge_ a racing sled for 1 or 2 people that is ridden with the rider or riders lying on their backs
18. _commemorative_ preserving or honoring the memory of some person or event
19. _biathlon_ a competing that combines cross-country skiing and rifle shooting
20. _hurdles_ race in which the runners jump over barriers
21. _international_ between or among nations
22. _challenge_ to call to a game or contest
23. _qualifying_ make fit or make competent; preparing
24. _triathlon_ an athletic contest in which participants compete without stopping in three successive events, usually long-distance swimming, biking, and running
25. _Olympian_ a participant in the Olympic Games

© Mark Twain Media, Inc., Publishers          100